# Unlikely Hero
# Om Puri

A poor village boy who held on to his dream of becoming an actor, Om Puri conquered the film industry by his raw talent and gritty perseverance.

Lotus Collection



First published in India in 2009
First paperback edition published in 2010
Third impression, 2024

The Lotus Collection
An imprint of
Roli Books Pvt. Ltd.
M-75, Greater Kailash II Market, New Delhi 110 048
Phone: ++91 (011) 4068 2000
info@rolibooks.com
www.rolibooks.com

Also at Chennai & Mumbai

Front cover image: Jagdish Mali
Design: Supriya Saran
Production: Naresh Nigam & Naresh Mondal

ISBN: 9788174368041

Printed in India at Repro India Ltd., Mumbai.

In a shot from *The Ghost and the Darkness*, in which Om Puri played the chief of the Indian workers' union.

Unlikely Hero

# Om Puri

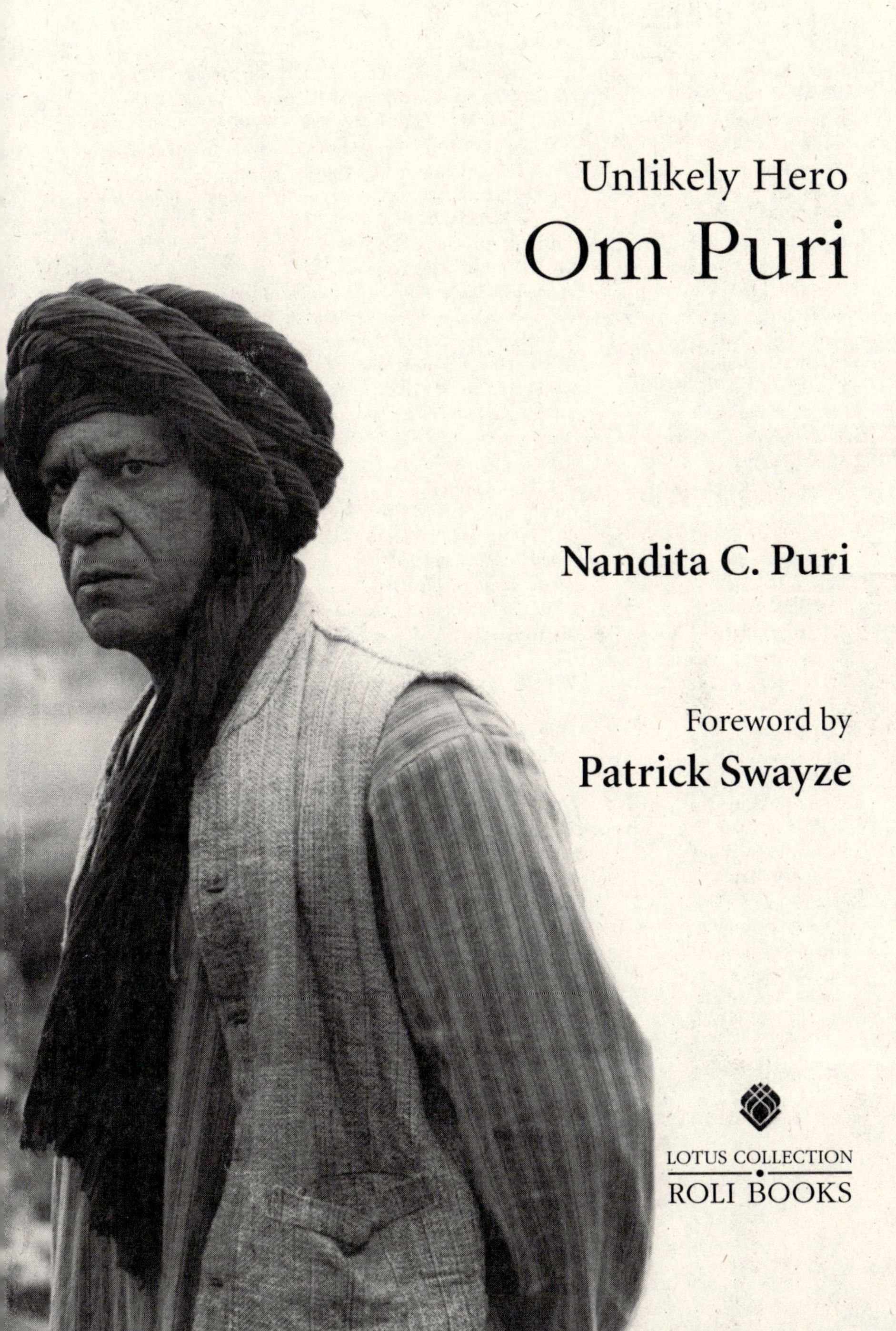

**Nandita C. Puri**

Foreword by

**Patrick Swayze**

LOTUS COLLECTION
ROLI BOOKS

**OTHER LOTUS TITLES**

| | |
|---|---|
| Anil Dharker | *Icons: Men & Women Who Shaped Today's India* |
| Aitzaz Ahsan | *The Indus Saga: The Making of Pakistan* |
| Ajay Mansingh | *Firaq Gorakhpuri: The Poet of Pain & Ecstasy* |
| Amarinder Singh | *The Last Sunset: The Rise & Fall of the Lahore Durbar* |
| Aruna Roy | *The RTI Story: Power to the People* |
| Ashis Ray | *Laid to Rest: The Controversy of Subhas Chandra Bose's Death* |
| Bertil Falk | *Feroze: The Forgotten Gandhi* |
| Brij Mohan Bhalla | *Kasturba Gandhi: A Biography* |
| Harinder Baweja (Ed.) | *26/11 Mumbai Attacked* |
| Harinder Baweja | *A Soldier's Diary: Kargil – The Inside Story* |
| Ian H. Magedera | *Indian Videshinis: European Women in India* |
| Kunal Purandare | *Ramakant Achrekar: A Biography* |
| Lakshmi Subramanian | *Singing Gandhi's India: Music and Sonic Nationalism* |
| M.J. Akbar | *Blood Brothers: A Family Saga* |
| Maj. Gen. Ian Cardozo | *Param Vir: Our Heroes in Battle* |
| Maj. Gen. Ian Cardozo | *The Sinking of INS Khukri: What Happened in 1971* |
| Madhu Trehan | *Tehelka as Metaphor* |
| Manish Pachouly | *The Sheena Bora Case* |
| Moin Mir | *Surat: Fall of A Port Rise of A Prince Defeat of the East India Company in the House Of Commons* |
| Monisha Rajesh | *Around India in 80 Trains* |
| Noorul Hasan | *Meena Kumari: The Poet* |
| Prateep K. Lahiri | *A Tide in the Affairs of Men: A Public Servant Remembers* |
| Rajika Bhandari | *The Raj on the Move: Story of the Dak Bungalow* |
| Ralph Russell | *The Famous Ghalib: The Sound of my Moving Pen* |
| Rahul Bedi | *The Last Word: Obituaries of 100 Indian who Led Unusual Lives* |
| R.V. Smith | *Delhi: Unknown Tales of a City* |
| Salman Akthar | *The Book of Emotions* |
| Sharmishta Gooptu | *Bengali Cinema: An Other Nation* |
| Shrabani Basu | *Spy Princess: The Life of Noor Inayat Khan* |
| Shahrayar Khan | *Bhopal Connections: Vignettes of Royal Rule* |
| Shantanu Guha Ray | *Mahi: The Story Of India's Most Successful Captain* |
| S. Hussain Zaidi | *Dongri to Dubai* |
| Sunil Gupta and Sunetra Choudhury | *Black Warrant: Confessions of a Tihar Jailer* |
| Thomas Weber | *Going Native: Gandhi's Relationship with Western Women* |
| Thomas Weber | *Gandhi at First Sight* |
| Vaibhav Purandare | *Sachin Tendulkar: A definitive biography* |
| Vappala Balachandran | *A Life In Shadow: The Secret Story of ACN Nambiar – A Forgotten Anti-Colonial Warrior* |
| Vir Sanghvi | *Men of Steel: India's Business Leaders in Candid Conversation* |

FORTHCOMING TITLES

| | |
|---|---|
| Géraldine Lenain | *The Last Maharaja of Indore: Yeshwant Rao Holkar II – Aesthete, Patron, and Tragic Prince* |

Ishaan, six months old, resting peacefully on top of his Baba's tummy.

For Ishaan . . .

A legacy you will cherish

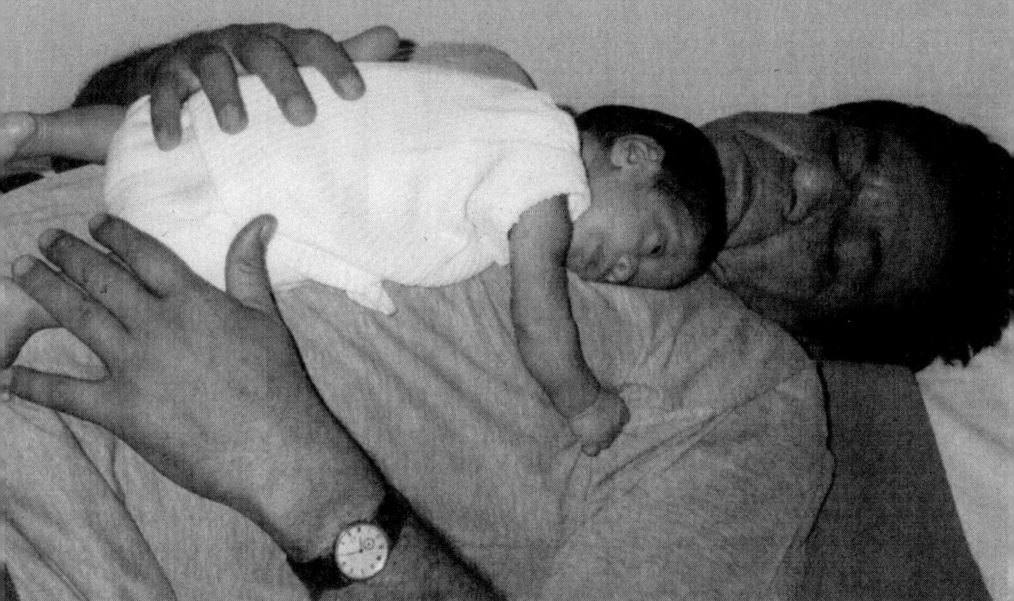

Om played a variety of roles from the beginning of his career. This one of an untouchable, Dukhi, in *Sadgati* by Satyajit Ray won him critical acclaim.

# Contents

# Foreword

I first met Om Puri during *City of Joy* in 1991 in Calcutta where we spent a lot of time, especially with me listening to him. It was an amazing experience for me as he was truly an Indian version of my father. They have incredibly similar looks.

What also drew me to him was his silent strength and power. I listened to his life stories and in many ways our life became mirrored in the film. We learned a great deal from each other. We both have overcome incredible odds. Both of us have gone through in life what most people don't know. Therefore, I am so happy that now his story will be told and I am looking forward to reading it.

In *City of Joy*, Om was my pied piper who helped me understand India in every way. As an actor he has such diversity and depth. You look into his eyes and you read volumes – that is the kind of power he has as an actor. This intensity makes him the master of mystical roles, which he excels in. Om's entire journey can be read in his face and he adds a layer of credibility and passion to every role he essays. Whether people casting in Hollywood knew it or not, they were casting a real human being, not merely an actor. He embodies the idea that true heroism lies in the quality of how you survive your daily struggle. To me he is my true guru.

I always make sure I research on those I work with. So I did an Om Puri film festival back then before embarking on *City of Joy*. I was moved by his role in Satyajit Ray's film, *Sadgati* and some others. So when it came up for Om to do Hasari Pal, it made complete sense.

In the process, Om taught me to move through the world with the dignity we all possess. I know I sound esoteric while talking about this man, but *City of Joy* truly changed my life. I came back to my country with a sense of shame of the bubble we live in and made a commitment to be like Om.

All you have to do is look at Om's face. He is a man who has been beaten up. You can see old scores in his eyes and you want to know more about this man the moment you look into his eyes. This sensitivity is counterpointed with wisdom and that is Om Puri to me.

He has an incredible sense of humour. The twinkle in his eyes lights up your life and this subtle sense of humour on screen is a very rare gift for an actor. This Om did in *City of Joy* and I am sure in many other films. It makes the performance layered. And I also got to find out what a good dancer Om was when we all had a couple of Indian beers. It evoked a lot of laughter.

I think I have done a great deal of talking about his strengths. I don't think I saw a weakness. This man was Hasari Pal. He became his role. I don't think there was ever a false moment I could detect as it wasn't there. We had such a compatible connection as friends.

The thing I was most amazed about Om was that he has lived a life that could have produced a bit of rage but he somehow transformed it into a great deal of love. It exudes from him and it is contagious. And that perhaps is the reason he became the big brother I never had in my real life. We did not act in the film, but continued our dialogue and it just happened to be the dialogue in the film!

The biggest thing I found working with Om as an actor is that he gives all of himself and with no fear, no defence, no justification. And that is remarkable in an actor. Hasari Pal is the core of *City of Joy* and I felt he deserved at least a nomination at the Academy Awards.

*City of Joy* is truly the story of Hasari Pal where the character is seen through the Western eyes of Max Lowe. And it is really how it went. The first day when I was working in Mother Teresa's home for the dying, I realized that I was the one to be truly pitied, not the dying. Because I got so much from life and did so little with it. And Om helped me in this endeavour of mine.

Patrick Swayze
New York, USA

# In Appreciation

In the fledgling days of his movie career, Om Prakash Puri, Padmashree, OBE (to use his full name and honorifics), was struck by severe doubts over whether he would be confused with and perhaps lose his identity to Om Shivpuri, former theatre doyen and unremarkable character actor in countless Hindi films. So our Om considered adopting a pseudonym! My two suggestions, 'Vinamra Kumar' and 'Antim Khanna' were rather impatiently turned down.

Then the time came for the hard decision. 'Prakash' was out for obvious reasons. Despite good old Amrish still being very much around, the 'Puri' could possibly pass. And so Om sweet Om had to change. Trivia addicts will be delighted to learn that in one or two of his first films he was actually billed as 'Vilom Puri' and 'Azdak Puri', both names he considered and then wisely discarded, finally deciding that the one his parents thought up was indeed the best. And damn, he was right.

This anecdote cries out for a punch line and here it is. True in every detail. Shortly after Om had been accumulating the success and regard that had long been his due, Mrinal Sen shooting at a studio in Mumbai received a call from 'Om' asking to meet. A request Mr Sen happily granted until embarrassingly, Mr Shivpuri showed up instead! Om Puri and Om Shivpuri – only time will decide which one of them posterity will remember. But I think it is a foregone conclusion.

Om and I are similar in that we are not, either of us, 'gifted performers'. Being entertaining does not come easily and since we both have had to slog to make things work for ourselves, I think, at the risk of sounding more pompous, acting has acquired a slightly higher purpose than mere entertainment.

Our relationship started as students in 1970 and then went on to becoming that of rivals (for roles, not girls), it then progressed to colleagues and in spite of all, we have remained friends. He is one living person whom I have constantly envied for the courage and integrity he has shown.

We used to be different actors then but now we have a lot of similarities. He used to be the hardworking one among us and I used to take my abilities for granted. Now it is the other way round to an extent.

Yet we have a healthy regard for each other and I am closer to him than either of my brothers.

When I first met him at the auditions at NSD, we appreciated but also envied each other. In a healthy way though. When I saw him perform in the lead in *Ibaragi*, a Japanese play, it was a revelation. At that point in time Om was an introvert, quiet. In the play he was cast in a flamboyant role which was completely opposite to his character. It first opened my eyes to him when I saw the magic in his performance on stage. It killed my envy and jealousy and made me, albeit grudgingly, admire his performance. It also opened my eyes to the kind of performance that could be achieved from him.

I have watched with fascination since 1970, not only Om's struggle to master his craft, but also his unending generosity with money, time and affection, and needless to say, I have been more inspired by him than any other living person. He often credits me with having goaded him to move to Mumbai and movies, a compliment I happily accept. But the simple fact is that the movies would have found him had he still been working in the State Bank of Patiala!

The story of Om Puri is in fact every struggling actor's fantasy: that a thoroughly ordinary guy can get ahead with nothing but good talent as godfather, hard work as insurance and the best of intentions as guide.

I often wonder how Om feels to be considered Amrish Puri's son or brother. Or for that matter he is sometimes mistaken for me! I, in turn, have more than once been asked if I am him or Amol Palekar or

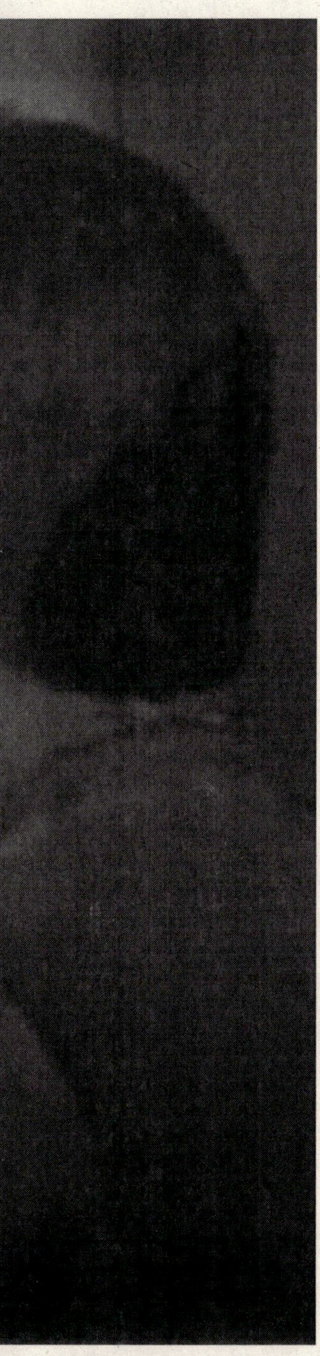

Girish Karnad. Makes you wonder if people actually look at performers closely at all or promptly lump them together. I daresay someone who knows little of cricket would easily mistake Zaheer Khan for Irfan Pathan! Though how could anyone, who has seen the face of Om Puri in *Aakrosh*, so easily mistake him for anyone else, I am at a loss to figure out.

The gradual metamorphosis, to which I have been a close witness, of O.P. Puri to Om Puri – from the scrawny, pockmarked adolescent underdog with hungry eyes and an iron will, living in a corridor with a stove, a saucepan and a few books into a significant, somewhat paunchy and a very prosperous player in the international acting scene – is the sort of stuff about which ballads were sung in the old days.

Om, however, has to make do with a doting wife recording his numerous accomplishments. In prose.

Naseeruddin Shah
Mumbai, India

Naseeruddin Shah as Om's co-actor in Govind Nihalani's debut film, *Aakrosh* written by Vijay Tendulkar. Om played a mute tribal man, Lahanya Bhiku, which impressed the best names of the industry.

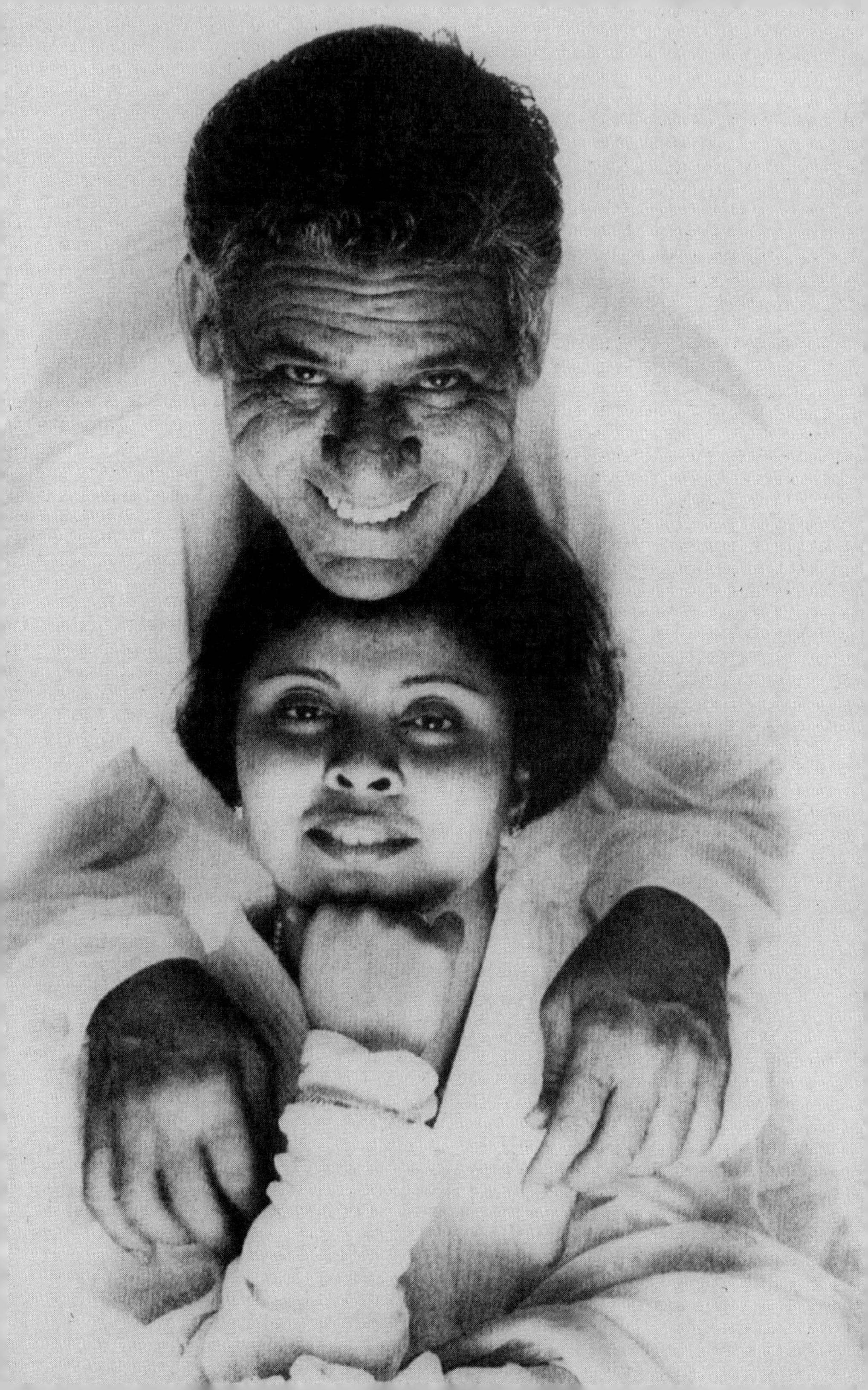

# Preface

It is always a difficult task to write a biography. Be it from a historical perspective or otherwise. Official or unofficial, authorized or unauthorized. A biography is a relative subject and hence its objectivity is always questioned.

It becomes doubly difficult when the subject of your biography is related to you. Like your parents, siblings or children. Or even friends. And it increases manifold when the subject happens to be your spouse! That too a spouse with very definite ideas of what should be written in his biography, who should be included and who should be excluded!

The idea of a biography on Om Puri stemmed many years back, when I first met him in Kolkata (then Calcutta), on the sets of *City of Joy*, where I had gone to interview him for the *Telegraph*. The idea was his and listening to stories of his childhood got me really charged. 'My life story is almost like Sir Charles Chaplin's … an amazing growth history,' Om had boasted then. 'Sure to be a bestseller.' Well almost, I thought to myself, and despite my hero-worship perspective of Om then, was not fully convinced about it.

Fortunately or unfortunately for us, the project did not materialize. The daunting task of a biography for a cub reporter was immense. Besides, I got involved with many other things, including the subject himself, to give it any serious thought. Thus it was pushed to the backburner.

In 1993, we got married. After the initial heady years of matrimony, Om did drop a hint to me of going ahead with the biography. Again, I

Facing page: Om with his wife, Nandita.

wondered whether I would be able to do justice to the biography without being prejudiced – in both the good and the bad sense. And so the project was abandoned a second time, while I devoted myself to running a home and writing prolifically.

Meanwhile, professionally Om rose to great heights, both in India and abroad. He was inundated with national and international awards including the Padma Shri and was made an Officer of the Order of the British Empire.

By 2002, the intervening years of writing and reporting had honed my skills in both word-flow and objectivity. So when the publishers approached me to write a biography on my husband, this time I considered it seriously. But lo and behold! This time the subject backed out.

'No,' said Om vehemently. 'You cannot write my biography now. Because you will not be objective.'

'Trust me,' I reasoned.

'No,' he seemed very hesitant. 'Why did it take you so long to decide on it?'

'Because I would not have been objective then. Besides, I did not want to write a biography on you that would be sponsored by you. It would lose its honesty,' I said.

'In that case, forget it.'

'Anyways, I am doing it,' I said, digging in my heels like any headstrong spouse would.

You may feel the book got underway on a wrong note. On the contrary, I think it began on the right one. A distance had been created between me and my subject insomuch as I could write about him independently now. And besides, being a journalist for more than fifteen years, I felt I could reveal facets of Om that were closest to his heart, and those he would have liked to share, due to our intimacy. When I visited his childhood place in 2003, I saw it anew through his eyes as he too was returning there after nearly thirty-three years. And from that point I took off on the life of one of the country's most well-known faces.

Yet, I believe that a good biographer does not sit in judgement on his subject but has the vision and clarity to expose the subject to the reader with honesty. The rest is for the reader to assess. At best a biographer can illuminate aspects of a life and through such glimpses string a story.

Every one of us has a story to tell. And to each of us our story is unique. But to bring this uniqueness to the reader and hold his interest is the task of a storyteller. And that is what I have tried to do in the following pages.

I have enjoyed every bit of writing this book. Om's friends, colleagues and relatives were very helpful and through their eyes there were moments when I got to view my subject from a different angle.

Then there were times when some people associated with him refused to talk. With the exception of a couple of gutsy women, others who were a part of his life were unwilling to talk about the past. Only Seema Sawhni stands out with her elegant grace in spite of joking that 'I cannot talk about the best parts to the wife'. There have also been those whom I may have unwittingly antagonized along the way as part of my job.

It is true that a spouse can lose her objectivity from time to time, fluctuating with the prevailing moods at home. Moreover, the canvas becomes so large that one can get confused about what to include and what to exclude without compromising the integrity of the work. One can be unduly kind or unkind, fair or unfair. So, for me it has undoubtedly been a cathartic experience.

On reading several other biographies I observed it is a person's work or art which is emblematic of the person. You cannot separate the one from the other. And yet, while reading a life story, often getting into the details of the artist's work can obstruct the narrative. So, in this book I have let Om talk about his work experience as separate sections while letting the main narrative of his life flow like a gentle stream.

Even if it at times does deviate from the above, I do not apologize. For this is more than a biography.... After all, it took sixteen years for this project to incubate before it was ready to see the write of day!

Nandita C. Puri
Mumbai, India

In one of the many different moods during the filming of Govind Nihalani's *Ardh Satya* named after a poem by Dilip Chitre. The film earned Om the National Award in 1984.

# Acknowledgements

The person I would like to thank foremost is Dr Shozeb Haider, without whom this book would never have happened. I have been sitting on this project for far too long until Shozeb gently reprimanded me and said, 'Put this top on your agenda and complete it. It will be a shame if someone else beats you to it with half your knowledge on the subject.' In other words Shozeb meant, C'mon, move your lazy butt. It did make me sit up and think … and write. Also thanks to Shozeb for helping me out with the numerous overseas interviews and patiently transcribing them for me in spite of his gruelling teaching schedule in Oxford. To you, Shozeb, I remain ever grateful.

To my son Ishaan, my comrade-in-arms, who kept reminding me, 'Is the book done?' That in itself was encouragement enough.

To my editor, Richa Burman, for gently yet ruthlessly cutting my copy to half! Thanks to you this book reads well and does not ramble.

To my publisher, Roli Books, especially Pramod Kapoor for germinating the idea and Priya for having the patience to bear with me. And to others at Roli at various points in time: Deepa Gahlot and Deepa Chaudhuri for prodding me, the latter albeit fruitlessly, and Supriya Saran for the fantastic layout.

To the late Patrick Swayze, for writing the Foreword. He was quite keen to read the book but it was not to be. I am indeed indebted to him.

To Derek Malcolm for graciously writing the introduction. (I feel he would be better equipped to write a biography on Om Puri.)

To Shyam Benegal for helping with the title; Anjum Rajabali and my gang of girls at F3 for gently spurring me on.

To my husband and the subject of this book, Om Puri himself, and his mood swings. His initial reluctance to participate made me determined to write. But later, his cooperation helped me write better.

And finally, to all who have contributed to this book. Also to those who have refused. To friends who wished this book well. And others who did not …perhaps that egged me on to give my best.

# An Introduction to Om Puri

I have been watching Indian films for nearly forty years now, often at festivals up and down India itself. And for most of that time I have seen Om Puri acting. I have never yet seen him give a bad performance, even in films that he himself might well say were hardly the best vehicles for his talents.

He is a remarkable actor, without doubt one of the best in India. He, together with half a dozen other performers, seemed to encapsulate all that was best in the outflow of talent of the seventies and eighties, which has now been cruelly stunted by circumstances beyond the control of its participants. There was a simple directness about his talent that masked its subtleties and gave a feeling that here was an actor who inhabited a character rather than took hold of those parts of it that suited his personality. So when he first came to the UK in an attempt to get good roles as the New Indian Wave was drying up, it was not surprising that I, and many other British critics – some of whom were discovering him for the first time – were pleased.

The result was three remarkable performances in *Brothers in Trouble, My Son the Fanatic* and *East is East*, which were every bit as good as those in such intelligent Indian films as *Ardh Satya, Mirch Masala* and *Aakrosh*. He was, of course, in Richard Attenborough's *Gandhi* and thoroughly deserved the honorary OBE he received for his contribution to the British film industry. Not many foreigners get that kind of recognition.

The British directors I have spoken to have told me of his outstanding talent, his quiet professionalism and his capacity for hard work on a role. They have also spoken of his generosity to less-experienced actors working with him. I am pretty sure their Indian counterparts would say the same thing. Satyajit Ray certainly did. 'That man has a wonderful voice and a great charisma. He ought to be a superstar. But then, I very much doubt whether he would accept the sort of films and the sort of parts that would make him one!'

Indeed, he probably would not. I remember an occasion, the 42nd Locarno Film Festival, when they were making a huge fuss about Bollywood (sorry, but that's a phrase Europeans use about song and dance spectaculars emanating from Mumbai). Like a fool I got up at a seminar to complain that if 'Bollywood' was all that Europeans recognized about Indian cinema, they were missing not only the work of Ghatak, Ray, Sen, Benegal and others, but turning Indian cinema into a mere purveyor of exotic extravaganzas.

Those in the audience immediately decried what I said as elitist. But then the deep and resonant voice of Om Puri came to my aid. He said that there were so few good and substantial roles available to him in India that he had to come to the UK to find some. That was a time when the New Indian Cinema seemed to have collapsed and Bollywood was not at its best. Goodness knows that not all British films are great but he chose well and certainly justified his move.

The insistence on selecting intelligent roles rather than going for easier success is the mark of most outstanding actors. And it is as difficult to sustain in India as it is anywhere else. I have lost count of the number of Hollywood stars who having appeared in blockbusters, and have asked me to suggest to them young filmmakers who would give them more intelligent work.

Om Puri has consistently sought these filmmakers out and as often sustained them. He is an extraordinarily honourable man in a profession that usually requires compromise and often begets disappointment. The only unfortunate part is that there are not too many roles for Indians in British films, which has restricted his work in my country. And only the fact that some of the best directors in India have such a hard time making what are non-commercial films has also perhaps restricted his work in his own country.

Yet, he remains one of India's best and an actor much admired in Britain too. Ray was absolutely right in what he said about him. Long may we continue to see and admire Om Puri's work, hopefully in good Indian as well as international films.

Derek Malcolm
London, UK
(Film critic, formerly with *The Guardian*)

# Born with a Wooden Spoon

Om Puri was born in Ambala (then in Punjab, now in Haryana) without a doubt, but there is a dispute regarding the date and year of his birth. There is neither any birth certificate nor any other record about it and the year could be 1949 or 1950. And his mother, Tara Devi always told him that he was born two days after Dussehra.

Later, when he joined school in Sanaur (near Patiala), his Mamaji or maternal uncle picked 9 March 1950 as his birth date and year. That stuck as the official date. Years later, around 1976, when he came to Bombay, Om decided to give himself a new birth date. He looked up the two days after Dussehra that year and decided to keep 18 October as his birthday and since then, that is the day he celebrates with friends and family. So at times he receives birthday cards twice a year.

It took him so long to decide on a birthday because he never had the occasion to remember or celebrate it throughout his school and college years, apart from the fact that his mother made *kheer* two days after Dussehra each year while she lived. No fancy parties or dinners. Just a bowl of simple *kheer* made at home to celebrate the birth of one of India's finest actors.

As many years later, his friend and colleague, actor Naseeruddin Shah was to remark, 'Om was born with a wooden spoon in his mouth.'

Om Prakash Puri was the youngest born of Tek Chand Puri and Tara Devi. He had eight brothers and sisters of whom only one survived – his older brother, Ved Prakash. All the rest of them passed away in

Facing page: A still from Richard Attenborough's critically acclaimed film, *Gandhi*, where Om played the role of Nahari.

Om as a Boy Scout in Sanaur Government High School, around the age of fifteen.

their childhood due to various diseases and lack of proper diagnosis and medical facilities. He does remember his older sister, Vedvati, who was married and had a daughter and came a visiting occasionally from the neighbouring village but she too died young. All that he remembers of some of his siblings are their names that he often heard his mother mention. Apart from Vedvati and Ved, there were Gyan, Kabli and Baby, not necessarily in this order.

His father, Tek Chand Puri was from Ambala where his grandfather, Sheo Prasad was a cloth merchant of sorts. The family was decently off but since neither Tek Chand nor his brother Kishan Chand was interested in the cloth trade, the business went to seed. While Kishan Chand worked as a cashier with Allahabad Bank, Tek Chand went on to join the army. Om does not recollect having seen his father in uniform – by the time Om was born, Tek Chand was employed in the railways as a junior officer.

Tek Chand also had three sisters and Om remembers his *buas* or paternal aunts fondly: Dulari Bua from Saharanpur, Rani Bua from Ludhiana and Maya Bua from Allahabad. Maya Bua's son, Raghukul Chaddha, is a good friend of Om.

Tara Devi's family came from Sanaur, a small village near Patiala, where they were farmers of some consequence. Tara Devi had a sister, Lajwanti and two brothers, Tarachand and Ishwarchand Kapoor. Om spent a number of his growing-up years with his maternal uncles' families.

Om's parents had had an arranged marriage and neither of them was very educated. Tek Chand may have studied till the eighth or ninth standard at the most, though he read and wrote fluently in Urdu, but Tara Devi barely went to school.

Om meets his close friend from school-days, Naresh Kaushal, after many years in 2007.

The first four years of Om's life were spent in Ambala in rented quarters and he recollects no family celebrations, no visits to the parks or to *melas* (fairs): in short, no entertainment. Tek Chand was very temperamental and hot-headed and kept losing his job every six months. It would take him two months to hunt for a new job and then he would lose it again in six months' time. Those were days of poverty and of a hand-to-mouth existence for the family.

Since Om did not go to school and had no fancy toys, he amused himself by playing basic games on the street like *gulli-danda* and marbles. Om's earliest memory is of playing with marbles by the gutter and every time a marble rolled into it, he would dip his hands to pick it up. And each time he dipped his hands, his mother would forcibly bathe him, irrespective of whether it was winter or summer.

Once some relatives had come home and given him five rupees to buy toys. Om was ecstatic and bought a red car which ran when turned with a key – a *chaabiwali gadi* – for a rupee and a half. Unfortunately, he had to return it as his mother thought the rupee and a half would go a long way to put food on the table, not a toy car!

Another childhood memory etched clearly in his mind is the time his hands were tied to the bed when the family was briefly living in Riwadi. He had got small pox and was always irritable and itching to scratch. In spite of his hands being tied, the pimples left permanent

Good at sports, Om was part of the hockey team in Sanaur Government High School. Seen standing on the extreme left in the middle row.

scars on his face, which in a way have become his trademark and add to his persona.

From Riwadi it was to Mullapur with his father and then to Dagdu. Though the family kept changing houses along with Tek Chand's jobs, the common factor that prevailed was poverty. Many a time, the family had to survive on the kindness of neighbours and relatives. Om remembers when his father had got home some money and the family was happy that there would be food in the house for a few days. But Tek Chand hung his *kurta* outside on a hook after dinner and by morning someone had stolen the money from the *kurta* pocket. This depressed the household for many days. From Dagdu the family went to Bhatinda where their quarters were next to the railway tracks in the railway yard. Om did not have any permanent neighbourhood friends, except for the sweeper's son with whom he used to play and whose company his mother disapproved of due to the caste barrier.

It was around this time that Om's love for trains grew. The trains used to be parked behind their house and Om would spend hours lying down or sleeping in the trains. Every time they moved, he would get up and leave, much like stray dogs sleeping under parked vehicles. His father took him in all kinds of trains and this became a lifelong love.

A tragic incident connected with trains, which is carved in Om's mind, was the death of his dog, Bisa. Bisa was a stray, adopted by his mother and him, and since they lived next to the railway tracks, Bisa would go to get food thrown off by the passengers every time a train came into the station. One day a neighbour informed them that a dog was lying in the bushes, his body having been run over by a train. When Om and his mother found out it was Bisa, Om could not eat for months, recollecting his decapitated body.

While the family was in Bhatinda, and Om was seven, he recalls the time his father, who was in charge of the railway store, was arrested on charges of theft. For four months, the family went through a traumatic period. He remembers an occasion when his mother and he were travelling in a train and his mother burst out crying. When the other passengers heard her plight, one gentleman got up and collected some money from the others so that the family would not starve for a few days.

Though it was a noble gesture on the part of strangers to help the family, Tara Devi's pain was much more than poverty. It was the humiliation of having to resort to such charity that pained her, especially since she came from a family of well-to-do farmers. Little Om also inhaled some of this humiliation then.

Two incidents which rankle him till date happened around this time. One was when he was molested by an elderly pandit with a white moustache, who made the little boy hold his private parts. Om realized that something was not quite right there. He did not complain to his mother but he stopped going to the pandit's house.

But the incident that brings tears to his eyes occurred when the family was told to vacate the railway quarters while his father was in prison. Since Tara Devi had nowhere to go, she kept pleading with the authorities. One morning they sent sweepers with a basinful of human faeces and threatened to soil the place if the family did not move out. They were forced to leave in a hurry and shifted to a one-room tenement for five rupees a month. Ved began to work as railway porter or coolie and little Om began to serve in a tea shop.

Thus, the age of seven Om started contributing in his little way to the family kitty, washing cups and glasses in a local tea stall. One

A reunion with Rajinder Kapoor (next to Om) and his family in 2003.

evening, the tea stall owner came home and was trying to make a pass at his mother since he knew Om's father was in prison. His mother stood up to him. All Om remembers is, the fellow while leaving yelled to his mother in an inebriated state, 'Don't bother to send him (implying little Om) from tomorrow.'

A year after that Om worked at a *dhaba*, where he did miscellaneous work and had to wash utensils at night. He was usually bone-tired at the end of the day, so he would hide the utensils beneath the ash in front of the shop and wash them in the morning. One day he was discovered and fired immediately: the owner was afraid the utensils might get stolen at night and couldn't take risks for a small boy. And so ended Om's short career.

Though Tek Chand successfully defended himself in court regarding the theft of cement from the railway godown, Om vividly remembers Bauji (his father) stealing bedding from a cousin in Ludhiana with no remorse whatsoever. He and Bauji had gone to attend a wedding and while the rest of the family was asleep, Bauji woke up Om, rolled the whole bedding, durrie, bed sheet and the *khes* (cotton quilt), et al., and urged the little fellow to tiptoe out before the rest of the household awoke. Om, all of ten, was shocked and acutely embarrassed about his father's deed.

Om virtually remained as a lone child with his parents since his brother, who was twelve years older, was sent to Ambala and then to Ludhiana to fend for himself. So it was his parents who created a strong impression on him during his childhood years.

Om recollects his mother as religious and god-fearing, a soft and gentle woman who barely raised her voice; a quality that perhaps Ved inherited. She even taught her children to treat animals with kindness. She called Om Guddu but generally did not show her affection by way of touch. She was a good cook and used to feed him his favourite *pila chawal* with *matar* (yellow rice and peas pulao) and *pakodiwali kadhi* often.

Even when as young as five, Om used to collect coal from the railway tracks and bring it home to be used as fuel. Once, Om and his friend found an egg. Om had never seen one but his friend explained that it was something edible. His mother would not let them enter the house with it but gave them an empty oil tin can and some wood. The boys lit a fire, boiled the egg in the tin can and then ate it with relish. It was perhaps the first time little Om had tasted any kind of non-vegetarian food.

The death of her children had taken a toll on Tara Devi and Om's enduring image of his mother was that of an 'old lady with grey hair and dentures', who looked twice his father's age. Om also remembers visiting his mother in an asylum in Amritsar much later, along with Bauji, where she was given electric shocks. He remembers her seated under a tree with a vacuous look in her eyes. The reason for her 'madness' was not clearly defined. Little Om also recollects his sister Vedvati having fits and behaving strangely from time to time. Vedvati was also treated in an asylum and died young.

Om's father was very loving towards him and tickled him often and affectionately called him Choochoo Bhukkha. One lingering memory of Om's childhood is when he visited the Golden Temple with his father. All of three or four years of age at the time, Om remembers Bauji carrying him on his shoulders as it was very claustrophobic. Perched on top of his father, he had a view of Darbar Sahib as Bauji walked through the waters. Nearly fifty-five years later, in 2008, when Om took his ten-year-old son to visit the Golden Temple, his memories of Bauji came alive.

Once, Tek Chand took Om away from his mother, and father and son went to Ambala. There, Tek Chand worked in night shifts. One morning when he returned home, little Om was fast asleep and would not open the door. From the following day onwards, Tek Chand would tie Om's feet to the window with a rope and leave for his night duty. When he returned in the early hours of the morning, he would tug at the rope and Om would wake up and open the door. Another time, when their tent was flooded, Bauji put little Om on the charpoy, put the stove on the plank and cooked a meal for his son and himself. Unmindful of possible fire hazards.

Though a loving father, Bauji used to get angry quite often – a trait Om inherited. Om realized later that his father's anger stemmed from the frustration of not earning and being able to support his family. Bauji would often tell Om's mother to get some financial help from her brothers, who were well-off, but her refusal would anger him further and he would hit her.

Om remembers the slap he received from his father on one such occasion. Bauji had slapped his mother. Not knowing what else to do, Om kicked the utensils which broke the mud *chulah* or stove. Bauji's big hand landed heavily on Om's cheek.

Om's feelings for Bauji almost broke down when he saw him beat his mother. Many years later, long after his mother was dead, when Om was making *phulkas* (fluffy unleavened bread) at home, he saw tears rolling down Bauji's eyes. When he asked him the reason, Bauji replied that it reminded him of his mother. It was at this moment Om felt some of his anger towards Bauji melt away.

Because of the lack of money, Bauji had to be frugal. During the mango season for example, Bauji would get mangoes but the half-rotten ones at a quarter of the market rate. Then he would cut and throw away the rotten parts and feed his family the rest. This sense of economy has been instilled in Om since childhood. And Bauji would call him *karmheen* (without luck) if he dropped food while eating.

Bauji was wont to do things at the spur of the moment. Once he was on his way to buy vegetables as Om's mother waited to cook for the family. Suddenly, he met a friend who was a guard in a train and on an impulse took off to Patiala with him without so much as informing anyone. Yet another time, he took young Om, who was then in eighth standard, to the army mess and handed him a glass of beer and told him to drink it. 'What is it?' Om asked hesitantly when he saw others around him laughing.

'Barley water,' was Bauji's prompt reply.

Overall, it was his father who influenced him the most, because to little Om, in spite of all his follies, Tek Chand was a symbol of strength – a fighter who had a lot of self-respect and hated subservience.

Patiala is a place most associated with Om, where he spent his formative years. Seeing the plight of their sister, Tara Devi, who could not make ends meet, Tarachand and Ishwarchand decided to lighten her burden and offered to take little Om under their care. But they spelt out clearly that Tek Chand was not welcome. Om would live and work with his maternal uncles' families and they would look after his education and he could visit his parents during the holidays. So around 1956-57, Om went to live with the Kapoor household in Sanaur, while his parents settled in Ludhiana. Tek Chand continued with his odd jobs at sporadic intervals.

When Om first arrived in Sanaur, only *tongas* were available as transport. Though there was no gas or electricity there, Om's first impression of his *nanke* (maternal uncle's house) was that of a big house with lots of grains and fruits around and enough wood for fuel. The family was well-off but they worked hard and lived simply.

Tarachand and his wife, Gomti Devi had no children, whilst Ishwarchand had three boys who were all older to Om. The boys were introverts but Rajinder and Devinder were nice to Om, though they were not really playmates. Ramesh, the older one, tended to be a little arrogant. Ishwarchand used to leave for the fields at the crack of dawn and return late in the evening. He ate his meals in the field between tilling shifts. Tarachand was a moneylender and had a shop in the main *chowk* in the heart of the village.

Om meeting Kishan Singh's family in Sanaur after thirty-three years. Om had stayed with them when he was thrown out of his uncles' house during school.

Om's duty was to fill water from the hand pump in the ground floor and during summer he had to sprinkle water on the *kutcha* terrace as the family slept there on summer nights. Besides, like his cousins, he had to wash his undergarments himself. Though he was treated with kindness, at times he did feel like a poor cousin. One difference he noticed was that while his cousins wore readymade vests of soft cotton, he wore the coarser hand-stitched ones. But these small things did not bother him much.

A delightful winter treat would be when the family made *pinnis* or *laddoos* and each boy was given his share which he kept in his personal jar. During the first few days, everyone would eat with a fury. As the *laddoos* diminished in number, they would start eating them frugally to make them last longer.

It was in his Mamaji's house that Om's acting skills were first noticed. Om always had a tremendous power of observation and during his free time, he would often wander away to the marketplace or to the railway station, stand in a corner and observe people. Then he would mimic the eccentricities and mannerisms of the people who had caught his attention.

Om, Nandita and Ishaan standing outside Government High School in Sanaur, which Om visited after thirty-three years in 2003.

One such person was the *dom* (keeper) at the village *samsaan* (crematorium). He had a spasmodic cough and would cough most of the time. Om used to imitate his cough very closely to the amusement of his cousins. They in turn told the elders and even they were amused by his act. Once some relatives came a visiting and his Mamaji asked Om to perform his 'cough act' in order to impress them.

Om was an extremely shy lad. But he could not defy his Mamaji. So he requested that the lights in the room be turned off, the old radio be switched on and kept at zero volume. The little light from the radio flickered on the shy actor's face as he performed to a dark room full of people. His relatives were quite impressed when he ended his performance and his Mamaji was proud of his shy nephew. Later, of course, enacting the most emotional or intimate scenes before several people in broad daylight would hardly matter to this shy lad from Punjab.

Om was nearly eight when he reached Sanaur and had never been to a school till then. At his age most boys were in the second standard. So his uncles sent him to a private school run by a very strict teacher called

Sadhuram. Sadhuram taught boys from the first to the third standards together so that they could get admission in a recognized school. In two years' time Om made up for lost time in Sadhuram's school. He remembers practising handwriting on a *takhti* or wooden slab and standing and droning multiplication tables in a sing-song manner: '*Ek dooni do; Do dooni char* … (One into two–two; two into two–four …)'

Two years later he was admitted to Government High School in Sanaur in the fourth standard. After that there was no stopping him. Om soon became the class monitor and kept that position throughout school. Besides being good at studies, he was good in sports like *kabaddi* and hockey, and was also a boy scout. During the prize distribution ceremony in the eighth standard he won prizes in almost every subject.

The principal, Pritam Singh soon grew quite fond of him. So, in spite of not being near his parents or being pampered too much at his maternal uncles', he did not feel deprived as he was pampered a lot in school by virtue of his merits.

Two memorable events during his school years were his trips to scout camp. One was the train ride to Allahabad, where the boys had fun besides learning to cook and wash utensils. This was when they were in the sixth standard. The other was at Taradevi, near Shimla. One day he and four friends decided to go out. All the boys were told to return before sunset. While returning, they spotted a temple and decided to go and visit it. By the time they returned it was very dark and everyone was worried. They were asked to pack and leave the camp. They apologized but they were not given dinner as a punishment, just a cup of tea. Hunger made them learn their lesson in discipline.

In school, his closest friend was a boy named Naresh Kaushal. They would sit together, study together, play together and even make some mischief together. Naresh was a bright boy and a good student too; he is currently the editor of the Hindi *Tribune* and is based in Chandigarh.

Remembering their times together, Naresh Kaushal says, 'Om had this habit of turning all adversities into positive situations. He was sincere and diligent in everything he did. Once while playing a soldier in a school play he saluted so hard that the stage broke.'

Another friend Om remembers was Kishan Singh, a farmer's son and junior to him in school. Kishan was a good sportsman and Om's *kabaddi* mate. But Naresh was his soul mate in school.

A fascinating incident in Om's life is linked with the first play he performed in school. In class seven, he played an army officer in *Himalaya Se Ooncha*, a one-act play. In the performance, he had to console his tearful wife while leaving for war. His wife was played by a *sardar* boy, Surinder, who was his batch mate.

Years later, in 1982, Om had to leave for Ahmedabad urgently from Mumbai. He caught a cab from Bandra to Bombay Central and told the driver to rush. When Om got off at the station and paid the driver, he turned towards Om and said, 'Guddu?'

Peering at the man's face beneath the thick beard, Om blurted out, 'Surinder?'

Thus the two long-lost actors met each other at a railway station in Mumbai, making so many Hindi-film fantasies seem real!

Surinder, who used to stay at Sion Kohliwada at the time, came to visit Om with his entire family. They have been in touch since.

~

When he was fourteen years old and in the ninth standard, a turning point came in Om's life. One summer night, as the family was sleeping out on the terrace, Om noticed his Chhoti Maami sleeping with her midriff exposed. He had been getting attracted towards her for a while and that night his reins snapped. He reached out and caressed his aunt's exposed tummy. She just turned away and muttered angrily. Next morning when Om woke up, his uncle Tarachand just glared at him and gave him a tight slap across his face without saying a word. He was told to pack his bags and Ramesh was given the charge of dropping him home to Ludhiana.

In Ludhiana, Om sulked for a while though his parents did not say anything. Om was keen to go back as he wanted to complete the rest of his education. A few days later, his brother Ved took him to Sanaur and tried to persuade his uncles. They remained adamant but Om too refused to return to Ludhiana. It was vacation time and school was closed, so Om literally had nowhere to stay. He persuaded the school *chowkidar*, Jethu, to let him in and he slept in the verandah. While he stayed there with all his worldly belongings in a tin trunk, Naresh Kaushal brought him food from home everyday.

When school reopened, Pritam Singh again tried to persuade his uncles to take him back but to no avail. Om was told to find his own lodgings. He then moved into Kishan Singh's house and helped with the farm work. He also took up tuitions after school and managed to support himself with the seventy-odd rupees he earned each month, after paying a rent of twenty rupees to Kishan. He used to look forward to little snacks at his students' houses, like a cup of tea and biscuits or *parathas* and white butter. Soon, he managed to buy a second-hand cycle with his meagre savings. During these times, Naresh also helped him out financially. But these tuitions took their toll on his studies. Despite being a rank-holder in school, he only managed to secure a second division in his matriculation examination.

From that early age, when fate left him on his own, Om learned the value of hard work. In spite of having to live by himself, he remains grateful to his uncles till date. If it had not been for them, Om would not have gone to school. Also, if his uncles had not thrown him out, he would have been an overseer (he had often heard them discuss plans for his future) somewhere in Patiala. And would never have made it to drama school.

Interestingly, Om insists his earliest ambition was of becoming a soldier. The incident which moved him and a lot of his contemporaries to join the army was when soon after the 1965 war with Pakistan, over 200 army jawans marched through the streets of Ludhiana in a victory procession. The grand parade inspired the fifteen-year-old to become a *fauji*. He applied for the entrance but his father could not afford the training it required, so his dream could not be realized.

But the glamour of celluloid beckoned him too. In the ninth standard he saw an advertisement in a vernacular daily asking for youngsters to audition for a film role. Om applied. He got a colourful postcard asking entrants to come for the audition in Lucknow and pay fifty rupees to participate in it. Fifty rupees was a huge sum those days and Om had neither that nor the return fare to Lucknow. So his celluloid dreams had to end then and there. The film, which was released a few years later, was called *Jiyo Aur Jeeney Do* (Live and Let Live).

# In the Wings

Khalsa College in Patiala was where Om took up an arts course in 1967. For Om, college was something he did as a part of life's ritual. His whole attitude was '*kisi tarah* BA *ho jayein* (I must become a graduate somehow)'. He survived by giving tuitions and also worked as a lawyer's *munshi* or clerk, which fetched him eighty rupees a month. After eight months, when the lawyer, Guptaji, did not give him two days' leave to perform in a college play, Om chucked the job and went on to play the lead in *Samundar Paar*. Some of his college mates told the principal who offered him the job of a lab assistant in his college, which now earned him forty rupees more.

But the defining moment in his life came during the college youth fest in the first year. This proved to be vital and spelt out the direction his career was to take.

Harpal Tiwana, the father of modern Punjabi theatre, was instrumental for the turnaround in Om's career. During the youth fest in Khalsa College, Tiwana first saw Om perform in *Anhonee*, a Punjabi play by Kapoor Singh Ghuman, where he had a parallel lead. Tiwana, who ran the theatre group Punjab Kala Manch (or just Manch), was impressed and invited the young lad to join him. When the latter was a bit hesitant because of financial constraints, Tiwana offered him a salary of hundred and fifty rupees per month.

The job entailed – apart from doing sundry jobs at the Tiwana household like fetching eggs and grocery from the market and babysitting his daughter Luna – organizing rehearsals and making

Facing page: A photo taken during Om's Punjab Kala Manch days. The photograph was circulated for film selection.

and serving tea to the actors. Mainly due to financial constraints Om had abandoned all hope of acting or joining films. Being pragmatic since childhood, he had decided to pursue a vocation which would sustain him, instead of trying to chase impossible dreams.

But the acting bug, especially in films, continued to tease him. Whenever he could afford it, he saw as many films as possible in the three theatres on Patiala's Mall Road: Capital, Malwa and Phool. He mainly watched the popular Hindi films of the day and his favourite actors then were Balraj Sahni and Dilip Kumar for their tragic broodiness and the singing-dancing Bengali boys, Joy Mukherji and Biswajeet for their kiss curls and chocolate-boy looks. Of course, today he laughs sheepishly if reminded of being a big fan of the latter two and brushes it off as 'only a passing phase'.

So when Tiwana invited him to join his theatre group, Om jumped at the offer. Harpal Tiwana did not come from an artistic background himself. His father was a police officer and the Tiwanas had been well-to-do farmers for generations. Harpal belonged to one of the earliest batches that graduated from the National School of Drama (NSD) where he had learnt the art of stagecraft.

About the role he played in his career, Om says, 'To me Harpal Tiwana was my first guru. He first introduced me to the seriousness of the medium. I am what I am today because of him. In a way his contribution was much more than my drama school professors later.'

Harpal Tiwana was dedicated to theatre even though, unlike in Bengal and Gujarat, it was not a popular medium in Punjab, where people preferred to spend money on films. Tiwana also had fewer resources at his disposal but he pursued his art with an ardour rarely equalled in recent times. Tiwana and his actress wife, Nina, whom he had met at NSD, were the torchbearers of modern Punjabi theatre. For them, theatre was a religion they followed devotedly. Every evening between five and eight, the members of the Manch practised in the Tiwanas' courtyard. 'It was like going to the temple,' Om recollects.

The next few years spent with the Manch and the Tiwanas were the most enriching for the youngster. He felt he was part of one big family, where there was no discrimination between members. From a middle-

Playing Doctor in Strindberg's *The Father*, with Nina Tiwana as Lara, in Central State Library Hall in Patiala in 1968.

class boy to a businessman's son to a sweeper's son – all participated and performed equally as part of the troupe.

Harpal Tiwana taught his students the dignity of labour and himself never shied away from any kind of work. He did manual work like fixing the lights, woodwork connected with the sets and at times even sweeping the stage floor. And he had an amazing way of conquering impossible situations. Since expensive spotlights were beyond reach for the Manch, he would take empty biscuit tins, cut out holes and put powerful bulbs through them. He got dimmers to control the lights.

Tiwana was immensely innovative and practical, two key points of being a good director. Om remembers Tiwana's quick sense of improvisation when they went to perform in a school in Dagshahi in Himachal Pradesh. The play was Strindberg's *The Father*. When they reached at night, they realized that the school had no stage. Tiwana quickly gathered all the dining tables from the school mess and tied them together with ropes. And lo and behold! A stage was ready.

It was with the Manch that Om first travelled out of Punjab as an adult. He went to Bangalore, Bombay and Pune with the Hindi play *Adhurey Sapne* based on Albert Camus' *Misunderstanding* and the

Punjabi play *Rattasalu*. He enjoyed the participation of the audience and their enthusiastic response. Inspired, he went overboard once. While playing the lead in *Rattasalu*, there was an incident where the police catches him wrongly and he is supposed to protest. Om jumped the gun and abused the policeman, mouthing lines that were not in the script. After the show, Tiwana reprimanded him gently about the wrong kind of improvisation. This was the beginning of his early lessons in acting.

Om recalls the train journey to Bangalore where the troupe had an entire bogey to themselves, organized by a talented actor called Jaspal, who was to be Om's good friend in the future. Om remembers making *alu parathas* for everyone in the train. Travelling with the Manch was fun and like a picnic for Om, a welcome change from the rather drab circumstances in which he was living. He remembers his first visit to Bombay around 1968 where they travelled with *Chamkour Di Gadi*, a Sikh religious play that they performed at the Shanmukananda Hall. A bike ride to Peddar Road is still one of his strongest memories of the trip as well as putting up in a small hotel in Dadar called Aroma.

Besides giving him exposure to the rich world of theatre and to life outside Punjab, Harpal Tiwana also introduced him to the slightly finer things in life. Like dining out. His first dining experience was at the Great Punjab Hotel & Restaurant in Chandigarh which was an expensive place those days. After a performance, Tiwana took the troupe out to dinner and Om felt a little awkward, though some of his more affluent Manch mates were comfortable in the small-town restaurant. When the finger bowls arrived with a slice of lemon floating in them, Om presumed the warm water had to be drunk after squeezing the lemon slice in it. Yet, he decided to first see what others did and follow suit. But when the toothpicks with the mint arrived, he ate the mint and holding up a toothpick, asked Jaspal, '*Yeh dakke kiske liye*? (What is this straw for?)'

Tiwana's contribution to theatre and in discovering and nurturing new talents was as important as Shyam Benegal introducing new talent to cinema. He was fair to all his students and was charming and charismatic. He had great convincing powers that came from within. He was magnanimous and even got a job for Om as a lower division clerk in the Punjab government's deputy commissioner's office where

Harpal and Nina Tiwana, graduates of NSD and the torchbearers of modern theatre in Punjab. Om joined their theatre group, Punjab Kala Manch, during his college days.

Om worked by day to earn two hundred and fifty rupees, and pursued theatre by night in the Manch.

Tiwana had a motorbike that he loved to ride. Om has taken many pillion rides on Tiwana *saab's* bike when he would drive him around the small city on odd errands, mostly trying to find sponsors for their plays. Tiwana was a totally focussed theatre person till his tragic death in 2002 in a car accident in the Kangra district of Himachal.

It was while working with the Manch that Om was able to make some more friends. One was Yograj, to whose house Om often went to eat when hungry. There was Jaspal, a short good-looking *sardar* who one day decided to chop off his long mane as he felt it was not getting him much work as an actor. For a *sardar* cutting off his hair is blasphemous and Jaspal camped in Om's rented room for a few days till his father's temper had cooled. Later, Jaspal repaid Om by typing out his NSD application form since Jaspal worked as a clerk in a bank. Jaspal and Om both applied to the National School of Drama together and on both the forms the address was Jaspal's: 24, Sevak Colony, Patiala.

Initially, Tiwana tried to discourage them from joining NSD as he felt they would end up as starving actors. It was alright if they had family money to fall back on, Tiwana counselled them, but coming from a poor background like Om's, he felt earning a livelihood, especially from Punjabi and Hindi theatre was going to be difficult. So both Jaspal and Om applied secretly without telling Tiwana. Of course Tiwana found out soon enough. When Jaspal and Om boarded the train to Delhi, it was their mentor Harpal Tiwana who came to the station to wish them luck and give them his blessings.

Meanwhile, Om did not finish his graduation as he got involved in theatre. During second year, he decided to complete his graduation through correspondence. In the meantime, he went off to Dulari Bua's in Saharanpur as his friend Subhash Sharma's father had got him the job of a canteen manager in the Post and Telegraph Training Centre. There, Om had to keep track of the canteen stock and count the *laddoos* and *barfis*. 'I never ate so many sweets in my life,' he recounts. A few months later he took the job in Punjab government that Tiwana had got him.

But he studied only till the second year and did not appear for the final examinations because by then he was headed to NSD. Of his teachers in college, he remembers a kind professor by the name of A.S. Dhillon who taught political science and the principal, Sant Singh Sekhon. Unlike school, his college years were not as memorable nor did he have any major love affairs.

The memory that is etched in his mind from his college days is the death of his mother, Tara Devi. One day Om got a call from his father, saying his mother was serious. He took the two-hour bus journey to Ludhiana and by then his mother had slipped into coma. She did not come out of it and breathed her last ten days later. She died due to complications from diabetes and lack of proper medication as the family could not afford the medicines the doctor had prescribed. This caused so much pain, hurt and embarrassment that one day Om went up to the terrace of the hospital and 'prayed to God that she should go instead of suffering the pain'. The next morning she passed away. She was around fifty-five at the time of her death. Om was eighteen.

The most upsetting part was that she died right before Om's eyes. The sight of her yellowed feet in the general ward and the doctor pressing her chest to revive her are scenes carved in his memory. He remembers the doctor shaking his head helplessly to tell him he could not save her. Om ran down to get hold of his father who had just left and was going across the road to have a cup of tea. Om called out to him and his father stopped. They looked at each other and his father understood.

It was after her death that Om realized he had no photographs of her. 'Before the pain of her death could register, the first thought that flashed through my mind was that I had no photograph of the two of us together.' He told his cousins and insisted they get a photographer. If there was no photograph of Tara Devi while she lived, her younger son wanted one at least in her death. So there are two photographs, one a close-up of her face and one with the family standing around. However, all this is not very clear and these are the only grainy remembrances of Tara Devi her sons have.

After his mother's death, Om stayed in Ludhiana for a few days with his brother Ved, who was working for a tent house owner. Later, while his father left for a little village next to Ludhiana, Om headed back to Patiala. And soon after, he took the train to Delhi.

# National School of Drama

National School of Drama proved to be a transforming experience for Om. Despite having a friend with him, his first six months in NSD were 'miserable'. The main cause was language. Having studied in Punjabi- and Hindi-medium schools, he could barely converse in English. It was not so much the inferiority complex that he suffered from but the sheer frustration of not being able to follow what he had come to learn. Though NSD had students from all states, most of them came from English-medium backgrounds. Even Jaspal spoke better English than Om. After the first few months, Om actually wanted to run back home to Patiala and maybe become an overseer (as his uncles had planned) or work as a clerk in a government office.

But the person responsible for averting this was Ebrahim Alkazi who was the director of NSD those days. Alkazi realized Om's discomfiture and sent a senior student, M.K. Raina to check on him. Raina befriended Om, found out the main cause of his discomfiture and told Alkazi. One day, Alkazi called and explained to Om that not knowing a language should not hold him back from pursuing his dream. 'You are hardworking and a good student and if at all you get stuck for words in English, just continue to speak in Hindi. Don't hold back. But you must read the English newspaper aloud daily, listen to the news in English and talk to your friends in English too.' This comforted Om; soon he settled down and began to enjoy NSD as he started to get good roles as well.

Now when Alkazi looks back at his shy student from Patiala, he says, 'I regard Om Puri as an actor of great emotional power and

Facing page: Om in deep thought about his next move as he plays the difficult role of Mohammad-bin Tughlaq.

Following pages: Playing the lead in the highly stylized Kabuki play, *Ibaragi*.

extraordinary range. He is an earnest individual, who with the searing intensity of his performances has raised the standard of dramatic skill in this country.'

Like the rest of his classmates Om used to get two hundred rupees as scholarship per month out of which forty rupees went towards school fees and seventy-five rupees for food, which included three meals a day. The remaining eighty-five rupees went on other sundry expenses like toiletries, incidental expenses, etc. He hardly managed to save much but whatever little he did save he spent it on seeing films and occasionally eating out with friends in Connaught Place, mainly vegetarian fare at the Glory restaurant.

Ebrahim Alkazi, son of a wealthy Kuwaiti merchant was like his earlier mentor, Harpal Tiwana: passionate about theatre. He was also a dedicated teacher and the roll call of his students reads like a who's who of the Indian theatre and film world. After Tiwana *saab*, it was Alkazi who Om looked up to as his guru. Alkazi was a hardcore disciplinarian, authoritative and very serious about teaching. He never missed a class, was hardly late and ruled his students with an iron hand.

A typical day in NSD began early for Om as he would go out to the open air theatre at 5.30 in the morning and exercise his voice. He also practised yoga. After a quick breakfast at the canteen, classes would begin at 8.30 a.m. and continue till one in the afternoon followed by an hour's lunch break. Then more classes took place till 4.30 p.m. After that there would be a half-hour break, just enough to have a cup of tea at the canteen before the students went to rehearse for plays till 7.30 in the evening.

The post-lunch classes were the worst for students as most would doze off, especially when professor N.C. Jain taught modern Indian drama. The students would fight over the last row of the classroom, where they could take their forty winks. If a sleeping student snored and another found it funny and laughed, Jain would holler, 'What is so funny?'

'Sir, *yeh so raha hai.* (Sir, he is sleeping.)'

'*To usko sone do* (Then let him sleep),' Jain would calmly retort.

Professor Alkazi taught Western drama and obviously his classes were the most popular as he was not only a learned scholar but an excellent teacher.

Om (on the extreme right) playing Pradyuman in the play *Suryamukh*.

The courses in NSD were structured quite sensibly. In the first year a student learnt all aspects of theatre: acting, direction and stagecraft. In the second and third years he specialized in a particular field. Om specialized in acting.

The acting students were engaged in physical activities like yoga, and dance and music as part of their training. R.B. Sharma was the yoga teacher who kept telling the students to eat healthy food and avoid fried food but himself gorged on *samosas* from the canteen daily. Sheila Bhatia, who taught improvisation and who was head of the acting department, was the butt of many jokes especially due to her heavy bustline. Every time she told the students to 'bring out their emotions' she moved her hands animatedly around her bustline and the students went into hysterics.

Sushil Chowdhury taught them music and Rita Ganguly taught them dance. Om and another student, Naseeruddin Shah, had no sense of tune. They were termed *besura* or tuneless singers. Many times during singing exams, the two of them were told to sing together as the professors did not want to suffer their vocal renderings twice. Professor Rita Ganguly could never get the two to dance either. Om hated dancing and had two left feet. Much later when Om had to match steps with Bollywood's ace actor-dancer Govinda in David Dhawan's *Kunwara*, Om regretted not paying much attention in Rita *di's* classes.

Though Om did not read much in NSD, he imbibed a lot in the classes about Western theatre, especially absurdist theatre. Alkazi encouraged his students to participate in other cultural activities apart from theatre to widen their horizon. The Triveni Kala Sangam would host a number of performances by the likes of Begum Akhtar, Amjad Ali Khan and others so that NSD students were exposed to the richness of Indian culture. Besides, Alkazi invited a number of theatre stalwarts from all over the world to teach at NSD. These included Brazilian Kaboos and German Fritz Benewitz, a Brecht specialist. Under Benewitz they performed *The Caucasian Chalk Circle*. Among the other plays the students performed with Alkazi were *Othello*, *Razia Sultan*, *Hiroshima*, *Three Sisters*, *Doll's House* and *Suryamukh*.

In Chekov's *Three Sisters*, Om played Vershinin opposite Suhasini Kale's Marsha. During a rehearsal of a love scene whereby Vershinin confesses his love for Marsha, Alkazi stopped the rehearsal and asked Om to perform the scene again. After Om's performance he told the class, 'This is the moment of truth in acting.' Om was touched by this remark.

Alkazi introduced the concept of a 'library period' twice a week in which the students had to sit in the library and read anything they wanted to. It was a way to cultivate the habit of reading. There was also a 'listening class' where you could pick up your favourite music and listen to it with earphones on. These classes were Alkazi's contribution to NSD towards making the students 'well-rounded' in their knowledge of the fine arts.

Another thing that Alkazi (like Tiwana) taught his students was the dignity of labour. Many a time he would pick up a broom and start to clean the classrooms or corridors if they were dirty, even though he would be impeccably dressed. 'Alkazi never wore a bush-shirt. He had his shirts always neatly tucked in,' recalls Om. His wife, Roshan Alkazi did the costumes for NSD plays and his children Amaal and Faisal hung around from time to time.

One of the different get-ups Om got photographed in for circulation among producers.

Alkazi tried to keep politics away from NSD. Once, the then prime minister, Indira Gandhi was supposed to come and watch a performance of *Razia Sultan*. She was a little late. Alkazi insisted the performance begin at the scheduled time, notwithstanding the absence of the prime minister of India!

Despite the initial discomfiture in NSD, Om made some lasting friendships during his three years as a student there. One of them was with Naseeruddin Shah, the other stalwart of Indian cinema of the eighties. Naseer came from a more affluent background. Hailing from Meerut, Naseer's family was well-educated and one of his brothers was in the army. According to Naseer's father, his youngest son was the black sheep of the family as he wanted to be an actor – not a particularly respectable vocation those days. However, the black sheep from Meerut was definitely more articulate and stylish and bright compared to the upcountry bumpkin, Om Puri. So Om was always envious of Naseer, especially in the initial days.

Their friendship began under the most unusual circumstances. Naseer being smart and confident always got to play the lead roles in NSD. This inspite of Naseer and Jaspal being students in the direction department. Once while casting for a play *Suryamukh,* Alkazi asked Jaspal to read for the lead role.For the first time the tongue-tied Om protested and told Alkazi that students of acting, like him, should be given preference to read for lead roles and only if they failed, the direction students should be approached. Alkazi was not used to being challenged but being a fair person asked Om to read the part the next day. After the class left, Om sat alone wondering whether he did the right thing by challenging Ebrahim Alkazi. As he came out of the class, he saw Naseer standing outside against a wall. Naseer came up to Om, looked into his eyes and whispered softly, "I knew you would speak one day." At that precise moment , Om and Naseer's friendship started, which was to continue beyond three and a half decades. There was many a time the two did not agree ideologically and even at times were envious of each other, but deep down their admiration and love for each other remains strong to this day.

Om's friends in NSD apart from Naseer were Jaspal, Jyoti Deshpande, Rita Puri, B. Jayshree, Rohini Oak and Jaydev Hattangadi. They spent time together, going out for meals and watching films. The boys and girls stayed in the same hostel, albeit in separate wings, and Om's roommates were Jaspal and Ramesh Pandey. Rohini remembers him as an extremely helpful person who helped ease her nervousness by explaining 'blocking' to her.

The first time Om experimented with narcotics was with Naseer. Om who was a non-smoker, enjoyed his few puffs, felt relaxed, but he did not really develop a taste for it. Much later, Om took to smoking cigarettes. Apart from smoking, Naseer introduced Om to non-vegetarian food. First he tempted him with a bit of mutton gravy, then later a piece of mutton and very soon Om started eating chicken and fish as well. Though he has been eating non-vegetarian food for years now, his favourite food still remains vegetarian, with spinach topping the list much like Popeye.

The other thing about Naseer Om envied was his way with girls. Being witty and charming, girls took to Naseer in a big way. He was

Om battling it out during a play at NSD.

the Romeo of his batch at NSD. Om was to have his own set of girls but he didn't know about it then. More about that later.

Among his seniors he remembers M.K. Raina and Nadira Zaheer. Raina or 'MK' was quite helpful to junior students and Nadira, daughter of poet Sajjad Zaheer, used to take all the newcomers for a meal to her house where the students would pig out on the kebabs. Later on, Nadira was to marry Raj Babbar, the well-known Hindi film actor. Babbar, like Om, also joined NSD via Harpal Tiwana's Punjab Kala Manch. According to Babbar, 'For us Om Puri was a star with the Manch.... To me he is what an actor should be: a sheet of clean white paper where you have the freedom to sketch what you want.'

The three years (1970-73) in the National School of Drama proved formative in the making of Om Puri the actor.

# Film & Television Institute of India

The Film & Television Institute of India, or FTII as it is popularly known, in Pune, was the next important location in Om Puri's life.

In 1973, after Om passed out of NSD, he – along with seven other actors – joined the NSD Repertory. His colleagues in the Rep at the time were Uttara Bahokar, Jyoti Deshpande and the late Manohar Singh. They were paid five hundred rupees a month and like a regular nine-to-five job the actors came in the morning, worked on a play throughout the day with aspiring or established directors of the time, and went home in the evening.

Most of his classmates had returned to their various states, so Om stayed as a paying guest in the apartment of a Bengali acquaintance, Sudip Chakraborty, who worked with the Punjab Estate. Among his circle of friends, Om was the only one who had stayed back in Delhi working as a stage actor. Naseer and Jaspal had meanwhile joined FTII to train further as celluloid actors. Though Om too was keen to pursue further studies at FTII, he did not have the resources.

After four months Om decided to leave the Rep as he realized he would get stuck as a theatre actor for life. Though Om enjoyed theatre and cut his teeth in acting on stage, it was nevertheless the silver screen that had a bigger appeal for him. Om's priorities were clear from the very beginning. The silver screen was and still is his only love; theatre was just a stepping stone to the big screen.

Life post Repertory days was tough for the budding actor as work was hard to come by. On stage, he got to do *Ghasiram Kotwal* with

Facing page: Om and his friend from NSD, Naseeruddin Shah at FTII. They were both growing a beard for Mrinal Sen's *Genesis*.

Rajindranath and worked in Bhanu Bharti's *Hamlet* along with Raj Babbar. The occasional Punjabi play for television and the once-a-month radio plays earned him some money but not enough to sustain him for long. Once again, he was in a hand-to-mouth situation. Somehow, he managed to pull through like this for a year and realized that if he did not leave Delhi soon enough, all his love for acting would vanish through the door.

On a holiday to Delhi, Naseer prodded him to go to Pune, but funds were the main hindrance that kept Om away. He applied for a Punjab government scholarship which did not come immediately. In the meantime, a friend from NSD, Neelam Mansingh asked her friend, a businessman, Jugnu Singh to sponsor Om. Jugnu agreed and on that assurance Om joined FTII. But Jugnu's funds never materialized. But that promise, however hollow, prompted Om to join the institute.

Om got in and was able to manage the two years' acting course in Pune due to the kindness of some friends and teachers. One such person was Girish Karnad. During the interview, students were asked to recite two passages, one of their choice and one that had been sent by the institute. Om's passage was Mark Anthony's speech from Shakespeare's play *Julius Caesar*. Om was good. But the interview board wondered why they should take Om as a student. 'He doesn't look like a hero, nor like a villain, nor a comedian. What use will he be of to the industry?' they chorused.

'That is not our problem,' Karnad, who was then the director of FTII, insisted.

'Besides, he has secured good grades in the interview and just going by his looks we cannot deny him admission,' said the late actor, Jayraj, echoing Karnad's sentiments.

Karnad allowed him to pay his fees later, when he was able to collect enough funds. During his first summer vacation, Karnad recommended Om to B.V. Karanth to play the lead in his hour-long children's film, *Chor Chor Chhup Jaaye*. That was Om Puri's first film and he played a vagabond. His first co-actor was a monkey called Ramu. He made friends with Ramu and sported an unkempt look to go with his character in the film. When the payment was handed to him, Om did

The expressive face which nearly prevented Om from getting admission into the institute as it did not fit any of the prevailing moulds for actors in Hindi cinema.

not know how to react. He had never seen so much money together – all of three thousand rupees! But he ensured that the money saw him through the entire FTII course.

His classmates included Suresh Oberoi, Rakesh Bedi, Satish Shah and Dilip Dhawan, among others. Naseer and Jaspal were a year senior to him and Naseer particularly took a devilish delight in ragging him as a newcomer. Benjamin Gilani, who had come to take his diploma certificate, also joined in the fun. They asked him to perform his audition piece and Om launched straight into it. What took Benjamin by surprise was that the entire speech was in Hindi! They made him perform it over and over again, reliving their thrill endlessly.

Some of the other students (who became 'stars' later) around the same time but in different courses, were Vidhu Vinod Chopra, Kundan

Shah, David Dhawan, Ketan Mehta and Saeed Mirza (all in the direction course), Renu Saluja (editing), Narinder Singh (sound) and Nadeem Khan (cinematography).

His first roommate, David Dhawan, remembers him as completely humourless, so much so that he insisted on changing his room! Now David recollects, 'I discovered him as an actor when we worked together in the 1990s in *Kunwara*, *Dulhan Hum Le Jayenge*, etc. We have indeed come a long way from the time I thought he had no sense of humour.'

His next roommate was an acting student Pradeep Verma who did one film later, Vinod Pandey's *Ek Bar Phir*.

A typical day at the institute would be to get up early and go for a walk or await your turn to the toilet. Then a hurried breakfast of *chai-pao*, tea and bun, at the canteen. Occasionally, if the budget permitted, an egg. Classes started from 8.30 in the morning and lasted till 1 p.m. followed by a lunch break that lasted till two. Post-lunch classes ran up to 4.30 p.m. and after a half-hour tea break, the students retreated to the main theatre for a film screening. A vegetarian dinner was served everyday at 8 p.m., with the once-a-week non-vegetarian fare.

During the financially tough years in FTII, Om depended largely on friends for even basic items like food and clothing. His classmate, Dilip Dhawan once gave him a silver suit which Om never wore. Bauji, of course, wore the pants later! A certain Chitle who was in charge of the canteen, often fed him without charging. Poona Coffee House in Deccan (a famous area in Pune) was also a place he liked to frequent with his classmates. Whenever he felt like a little change in food he would go and have a vegetarian Marathi *thali* for three rupees. And the first time he visited a Continental restaurant called The Place on Main Street for a sizzler was with his friend Harry Dhaul.

Since he could not visit Punjab, the only way he could keep in touch with his father was through letters. Bauji always wrote in Urdu and Om had to seek Naseer's help to have his letters read to him.

The Punjab government scholarship, that was supposed to see Om through the FTII course, arrived at the end of the final year. At that

Facing page: Om's first 'co-star', Ramu the monkey, in B.V. Karanth's film *Chor Chor Chhup Jaaye*, which Om did during his first year at FTII.

time he still owed FTII two hundred and eighty rupees and his course of two years was almost through. When the accountant asked him to pay up, on an impulse Om refused.

'You will not get your diploma certificate,' the accountant yelled after the fleeing Om.

'Doesn't matter,' Om replied. 'I have finished the course.'

Till date Om Puri owes the Film & Television Institute of India two hundred and eighty rupees. Add to that three decades of interest! Once in the '80s, FTII had sent him a letter asking him to repay the debt (minus the interest), the opening lines stating, 'By God's grace you are doing well ...' Om still refused to pay, if only for the impish thrill it gave him of owing FTII some amount. And of course he never got his diploma certificate.

Om was in the last batch of students that passed out of FTII's acting course (1974-76). According to Om, the FTII course structure was not well-designed. While at NSD the theory classes used to be intense, in FTII, no film theory or literature was taught. The student actors were taught cinematic techniques like action, scene movement, dance, and yoga for physical fitness. Apart from Roshan Taneja, who headed the acting department at FTII then, Om hardly remembers any other teachers. 'Some were ex-students turned teachers for want of a better career. The speech trainers were particularly bad. After NSD, it was frustrating at FTII.' According to Om, it was quite a frivolous course, structured according to the existing Hindi commercial film industry of Bombay; and to get a smoother entry into it was the main reason for Om to stay on.

Ultimately, film screenings were the 'only source of learning' at FTII. Om's horizon in world cinema widened as he got to see the classics and got acquainted with the works of master filmmakers. To the credit of FTII, it has a great film archive which introduced every important film genre and most of the master filmmakers, from Ray to Bergman, Fellini to Ghatak, Kurosawa to Bimal Roy and from Zanussi to Raj Kapoor, to its students.

Apart from that, Om learned a lot from discussions with like-minded senior students like the Marxist Saeed Mirza or Ketan Mehta in their rooms, which often extended up to the wee hours of the mornings over cheap bottles of country liquor. The favourite was Double Ghoda, meaning 'double horse', which came for eight rupees a bottle and often gave total value for money with at least eight drunks on hand. Once Om even tried to get 'more enlightened' and along with Naseer, Jaspal and Ketan Mehta climbed up a hill after experimenting with a potent variety of grass. Next morning, they came down the hill, Om none the wiser.

Om's sole crush at the FTII was a fellow acting student, Sohini Singh. But since it wasn't reciprocated, it began and ended from his side only. The students at FTII were often regarded in high esteem by the locals. One such was a local prostitute named Paro, who was very generous to these 'future stars'. Just the mention of the institute and her services were often rendered without any charges. Another person was Sheikh, who drove an auto rickshaw. He was mainly seen in front of the FTII main gate and ferried the students free of charge on most occasions.

Besides these minor distractions, Om doesn't remember much else from his FTII years. He did not even get many roles in the diploma films. Some of the diploma films he appeared in were Saeed Mirza's *An Actor Prepares*, Kundan Shah's *Bunga*, and other small assorted roles. Most of the direction students used to take actors from outside FTII in their diploma films and this angered the acting students. As a protest, Naseer and his classmates had once gone on strike. Classes had come to a standstill for three whole months.

It was during his FTII days that Om had a brush with the Indian prison system. In other words he served half an hour in jail. He was returning from Bombay to Pune and had a valid ticket for the Deccan Queen. Unfortunately, he missed the train and took the Mahalaxmi Express instead. When the ticket collector questioned him, he refused to pay up saying he had a valid ticket, never mind which train. He was taken to the police station. However, a fellow classmate, cinematographer Pankaj Kumar from Bihar bailed him out.

# Bombay 1976

In 1976 Om came to Bombay. The first place he went to was Naṣeeruddin Shah's PG (paying guest) digs at Santa Cruz. The place was called Martin Villa and it was behind the Sacred Heart Church. Naseer shared it with his friend Tikka Singh (also from FTII). After requesting the landlady, Om was allowed to stay for a week. But when the week extended to more than a fortnight, the landlady asked Om to leave. Naseer called a friend staying next door, Chawla, who was also an agent and got Om a rented PG accommodation in Bandra. It was in a little lane near St Andrew's Church named St Francis Road. The place was called Shelter!

Shelter was not your typical Bollywood beginner's abode. It was a rather luxurious place for a small-town boy to begin life in a megacity where millions come to realize their dreams. For a hundred and seventy-five rupees a month, he got a room with a bed, a cupboard, a table and a chair in a quaint little bungalow belonging to a Catholic family, the D'Souzas, which included a cup of tea in the morning. With the six hundred rupees he had in his pocket when he arrived in Bombay, he paid his first month's rent.

During his first few weeks in Bombay, Om used to have a strange recurrent dream. He dreamt he was a little boy playing with a ball on Juhu beach. A huge monster would emerge from the sea and approach Om in slow motion with a faint smile on his lips. He would ask little Om for the ball. Om would throw the ball in fright and run as fast as he could. During the chase Om's dream used to break. Analyzing the dream in retrospect, he interpreted the monster to be the high-rises in the city – for a small-town boy from Patiala, their impact was indeed monstrous.

Facing page: Freshly graduated from FTII, Om was excited as well as apprehensive about his future in Bombay.

But in the following months Om decided to make Bombay his home and workplace, his long-term residence. Luckily for him, Bandra proved to be a lovely beginning in the city. 'The Queen of the Suburbs' as it is called, Bandra was originally one of the fishing islands that constituted Bombay and has a quaint mixture of the old and the new. The area is still dotted with pretty bungalows belonging to the Catholic families who have resided in the area for generations, though a number of the older bungalows have made way for swanky high-rise apartments.

A walk down the promenade, sitting and watching the waves hit out at the rocks on Bandstand, a walk uphill to Mount Mary's Church, and sitting on the pew on a quiet noon in St Andrew's Church, were some of the things Om savoured in his first few months in Bandra. It was near St Peter's Church on Hill Road that he cast his first vote ever and was glad to realize that he was one of the millions who voted Mrs Gandhi back to power in 1979.

Another favourite pastime was having his morning cup of tea at the Yacht restaurant. He would sit and observe people there, especially a group of senior citizens who came daily for their cuppa. There used to be four or five of them and six months later Om noticed their mood had mellowed. He also noticed one less among them. Obviously, one old man had passed away.

Om stayed with the D'Souzas for a couple of years before he had to vacate the room for their son who was returning from Dubai. Om moved to the nearby Kerala Catholic Association (KCA) hostel where he shared a room with his former roommate from FTII, Pradeep Verma. During this time, Bauji visited Om once and stayed with him at the hostel, and Om also bought his first piece of property. It was a modest house for his brother, Ved's family in the suburbs of Ludhiana. It cost him thirteen thousand rupees, five thousand each borrowed from Naseer and Rameshwari, an actress and friend from FTII, and three thousand from his own savings.

Om's first assignment in Bombay was an ad film directed by Govind Nihalani for a packaging firm. He got the assignment through Naseer, who was also in the film. They both acted as factory workers and Om got eight hundred rupees. They shot the film somewhere near Mahalaxmi Studio and Om remembers his first fancy meal, a lunch out with Govind and Naseer at Shamiana restaurant, now Viva Paschim, near Worli.

During those early years a rather unfortunate incident cemented their friendship. One evening Om and Naseer were sitting at a small restaurant near Khar station, having just ordered dinner when Om suddenly saw Jaspal approaching Naseer from behind and strike the latter on the back.When Jaspal raised his hand Om saw a knife and before Jaspal could strike again Om grabbed his arm which was as hard as an iron rod with tension.Naseer bleeding ran out while Om struggled with Jaspal till the staff came in to mediate. The police arrived and took Jaspal away and put him in the lock-up. Though Om remains tight-lipped about the reason for Naseer and Jaspal's hostility, he is happy that he was able to save his friend's life then.

Not much happened for Om in those initial days. He survived on the odd job of a voiceover or a stray role here and there. In 1977 he acted in *Godhuli*, which was co-directed by B.V. Karanth and Girish Karnad. Another film he did during this time was *Shaayad*, which got him his first fan. He distinctly remembers the fruit seller next to Lucky restaurant in Bandra who told him, '*Aap ne bahut achcha kaam kiya*. (You did a great job.)'

Meanwhile, he decided to get himself a steady job that would at least ensure his monthly rent. His teacher from the FTII, Roshan Taneja, had opened an acting school in Bombay called Actors' Studio a few years earlier. Om went to Taneja who offered him to teach speech and movement on a salary of eight hundred rupees a month. Plus, he was paid extra for overtime.

Om taught for a year and among his brightest students in the school were Anil Kapoor, Gulshan Grover, Mazhar Khan, Surinder Pal and Madan Jain. Om remembers them as a bunch of enthusiastic young boys who would badger him with questions during the break. They often treated him to tea and snacks and even walked him to the bus stop in Juhu. They were the best batch that Taneja produced and according to Om 'they all made it in films'.

'Of all my teachers from school and college, Om Puri was the most vulnerable, innocent and childlike. As a teacher, he wanted to give so much that once he cried, thinking he had failed because he could not convey what he wanted to. It was a great pleasure to watch him enact and interpret scenes from old Bimal Roy films with honesty and sincerity. He was more like an elder brother than a teacher to most of us,' recollects Anil Kapoor.

On the other hand, Gulshan Grover has this to say about him: 'What I learnt from Omji is the importance of the subtext. As a teacher he was serious and later as a colleague, I found him jovial. He does not take his greatness too seriously and does not carry his attitude to the sets.'

After staying for nearly four years in Bandra, Om and cinematographer Gyan Sahai hired an apartment in Borivali, the farthest end of Bombay. Commuting became a problem and Om seriously realized this one day when he was shooting for a small project and he left the script home. He had to travel all the way and back, which took a major part of the day. After that Om decided to relocate himself to a more accessible area. He landed himself in the heart of Bombay, on Marine Drive's C. Road, overlooking the huge expanse of the Arabian Sea in a building called Ganga Vihar.

The owner of the apartment in Ganga Vihar was one Rani Burra or Chinna as she was fondly referred to. Chinna had passed out from FTII as a screenwriter and was senior to Om. Om also knew her husband Subhash Dey. Ganga Vihar was like a hub for upcoming actors, filmmakers and other assorted artists. Incidentally, the Bollywood legend, Amitabh Bachchan too spent his early days there, around the same time as Om, albeit in a different apartment. While in Ganga Vihar, Om started getting offers for bigger films. Om's first big break came in 1980 with *Aakrosh*.

He played the mute Lahanya Bhiku, the tribal who refused to speak as he felt he was wronged by society. In spite of a non-speaking role, Om's performance made critics take notice of him. Though Om ended up being offered roles of henchmen post *Aakrosh*, filmmakers did begin to see him as an actor with calibre. It was then that the legendary Satyajit Ray offered him a role in his telefilm *Sadgati*.

*Aakrosh*, based on acclaimed Marathi writer, Vijay Tendulkar's

Facing page: An early photograph of Om for circulation in film studios in Bombay. In Hindi cinema, appearances were as important in those days as they are today.

script was directed by Govind Nihalani. It was also Govind's first film as a director. He was an established cinematographer and Om first met him on the sets of an ad film and later on the sets of Shyam Benegal's *Bhumika* (1977), in which he had a small appearance. 'In *Bhumika* he played a small role but he did it with panache.... Somewhere in my mind I stored the fact that he is a fine actor.... In *Mandi* he proved his flair for comedy,' Benegal said later.

Though *Aakrosh* was not commercially viable, it did the festival rounds and won several awards. It also got Om his first accolade, the Filmfare Award for Best Supporting Actor in 1982. According to Nihalini, 'Through Om's face I could see a lot of tragedy, I could see Lahanya's history.... The unit was still after the shot as he made them feel that the anguish was real ... This kind of intensity cannot be manufactured or contrived.... Some actors are a dead giveaway with their body mannerisms. But Om adapts to the character.... One role I would have liked him to do is Sakharam Binder. It is as if the role has been written for him.'

The film had an impact on the commercial-film audience too. Om received several fan mails; the one among them he particularly remembers came from a young girl who wrote that she was moved by the plight of the tribals after seeing *Aakrosh* and it made her take up social work. Many years later, while filming in a village near Madhya Pradesh, an elderly couple saw and recognized him. They called out to him by his screen name, Lahanya Bhiku. It was a great compliment for Om.

One of the prestigious assignments he was offered during this time was Christopher Morahan's television serial *The Jewel in the Crown*. It earned him fifty thousand rupees with which he bought his first car for thirty thousand, a second-hand Fiat, 1953 model. He bought it in Pune and hired a driver to take him to Bombay. Though all acting students had been taught driving and swimming in FTII, Om was out of practice. Even for months after acquiring the car, Om could not reverse!

Sometime after *Aakrosh*, Om met Seema Sawhni, who was to leave a strong impact on Om's mind and thinking process. She was the first to open the doors to the small-town lad, leading him into some of Bombay's elite social circles. Om met influential people in arts and advertising through Seema, though he still was not the very outgoing sort. Slowly, he started to open up. He started attending parties and soon got into the routine vices of smoking and drinking. Smoking started with holding the odd cigarette at parties to 'look cool' and drinking began with having the odd drink at social gatherings to 'feel cool'.

Besides the socializing, living in Ganga Vihar was invigorating as he moved around Queen's Necklace, savouring the view and occasionally eating out at Mathura Dairy Farm. One early morning, while standing outside in the balcony, watching the huge expanse of the Arabian Sea, Om thought he saw Bauji standing across the road, looking up towards him. Om quickly ran down the stairs and crossed the road to greet his father. Bauji was not there. Om figured he had been hallucinating.

Later that afternoon, Bauji showed up unannounced at Om's apartment. When Om asked him whether he had been there earlier in the morning, Bauji replied in the negative. It was uncanny.

Bauji had always been a vagabond and he enjoyed visiting friends and relatives all over Punjab whenever he tired of staying in one place for too long. After a couple of visits to Bombay Bauji realized that at last his little boy had become a man, so he began to stay with Om more often. Soon, it became impossible to accommodate him in Ganga Vihar, so Om rented out a room at Bhagat Singh Colony in Andheri East, and Bauji came to live with him.

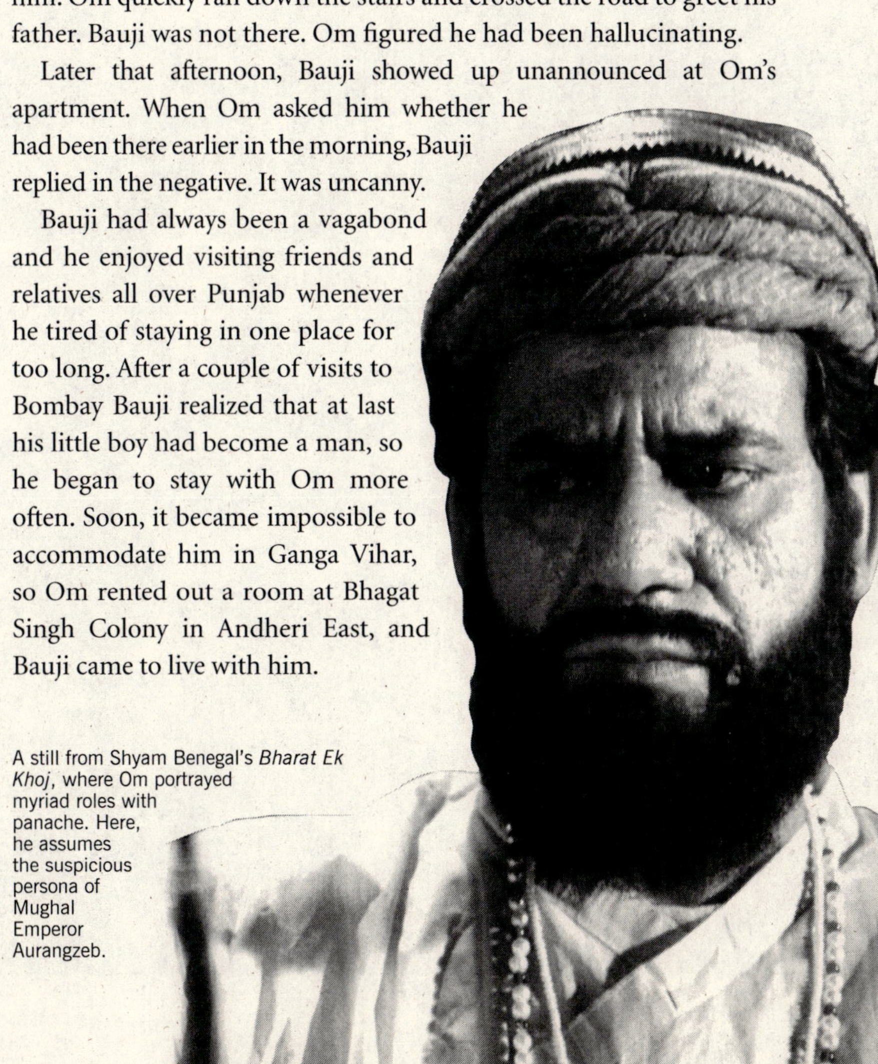

A still from Shyam Benegal's *Bharat Ek Khoj*, where Om portrayed myriad roles with panache. Here, he assumes the suspicious persona of Mughal Emperor Aurangzeb.

# Majma

Om had set out to Bombay from Patiala to conquer the silver screen. But it was easier said than done. Those days too, chocolate-boy good looks were in demand in mainstream Hindi cinema. So, except in the occasional New Wave films, where he had begun to get roles, it was doubly difficult for Om (who looked neither 'like a hero, nor a villain, nor a comedian') to get any part in commercial films.

After tiring of teaching in Actors' Studio, Om decided to turn to theatre. In Hindi theatre, actors performed more for the love of the medium than for livelihood, due to which it lacked professional consistency. At the time, there were only two credible theatre groups: one was IPTA (Indian People's Theatre Association) and the other was Theatre Unit. 'If I had approached any of the two, I would have had to stand in a long queue,' Om reminisces. So he decided to form his own theatre group called Majma, literally meaning 'a gathering', in 1978.

The founding members were Naseeruddin Shah, Rohini Hattangadi, Madan Jain, Attar Nawaz, and Naresh Suri among others. Actors like Ratna Pathak, Karan Razdan and the late Priya Tendulkar also performed for Majma.

Majma's first performance was *Udhwast Dharamsala* which was performed in Chabildas Theatre. Written by

Om during his time in Majma, a theatre group he started. Even though he excelled on stage, cinema remains his first love.

playwright Govind Deshpande, the play travelled to Delhi, Calcutta, Bombay and Ahmedabad. It was also the inaugural play of Bombay's famed Prithvi Theatre that was opened in Juhu in 1979-80 in memory of the late Prithviraj Kapoor. Om heard about it and knew Shashi Kapoor as he had done a small role in the latter's film *Kalyug* (released in 1981). Shashi sent him to his wife Jennifer. Jennifer did not want much hype and wanted a low-key opening with a good play. She agreed to stage *Udhwast Dharamsala*.

But Om had other ideas. He informed a few people from the local press to watch the inaugural performance and this gave a lot of mileage to both Prithvi Theatre and Majma. The show went off well except for a minor disagreement Om had with Jennifer, as she insisted not to charge the audience money. 'Just take a rupee from each person who attends,' she told him. 'If there are fifty people, take fifty rupees; if there are twelve, take twelve rupees. One rupee from each person.' Om retorted, 'How will you run your theatre then?' But he couldn't do anything about it.

During the initial days of Majma Om devised a novel way of collecting money, inspired by the late Prithviraj Kapoor himself. After each play, Om had a boy stand outside the theatre, holding a cloth where people dropped any amount of money they felt like giving. The boy was instructed never to look up at any person so as to avoid embarrassing him or her.

Another play that Majma produced was

*Bichchoo*, an adaptation of Molière's *The Scorpion*. It was directed by theatre director Ranjit Kapoor and travelled to the Middle East besides being performed in Bombay. During the Majma days, Om was staying in the KCA hostel. A couple of years after working in Majma, Naseer left to form his own theatre group Motley with Benjamin Gilani. In Benjamin's words, 'Later when Motley had its own production we had, "Majma presents Motley". Soon Motley decided to buy out from Majma and so the proceeds of one of Motley's shows, a thousand-odd rupees, went straight into Majma account. Thus we had two separate banners now. The irony is that whilst Motley is still active, Majma has died down. Still Om remains our founding father.'

It has now been almost a quarter of a century since Om gave up theatre. Though the urge is there at times, he hesitates. Sometimes, he envies Naseer who still pursues theatre in the midst of his busy film schedule. But Om has no regrets. 'Theatre gives you instant satisfaction as an actor as you connect with a live audience. But films have a wider reach and are socially more relevant. Look at *Tamas* or *Aakrosh*. Would I have ever been able to reach that kind of audience, in such unknown corners of the country?'

During the play *An Enemy of the People* that Om staged with Majma, a joint venture between him and other students from FTII.

Following pages: Om performing in *Bichchoo*, a Majma adaptation of Molière's *The Scorpion*.

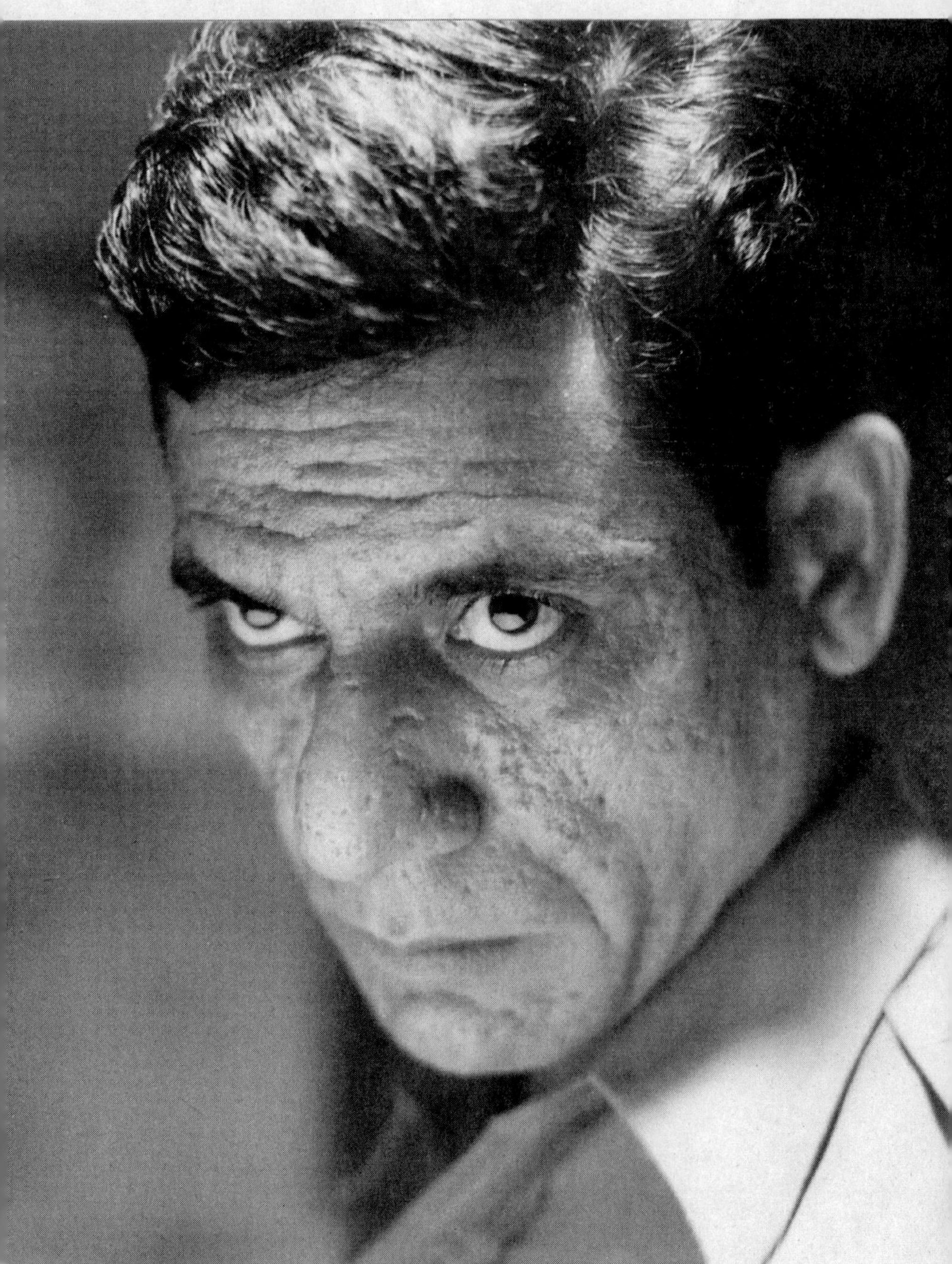

# Ardh Satya

There comes a time in an artist's life when one particular work becomes the hallmark of his genius. It represents the core of his work. Like Tchaikovsky's *Swan Lake* or Orwell's *Animal Farm* or Picasso's *Guernica.* In Om's case it was *Ardh Satya.* It not only established Om as the actor Om Puri, but also proved to be a major turning point in his life.

Govind and Om already shared a rapport and *Ardh Satya* was their second film together. A short story, 'Surya' – about a disgruntled cop, Anant Velankar – was the inspiration for the film. Written by D.A. Panvalkar, it was based on the true story of a customs officer in Bombay. Govind was excited by the subject and asked Vijay Tendulkar to write the script. Till date it is one of the best written screenplays in Hindi cinema. When Om heard Govind's narration of the story, he was excited beyond measure. For an actor it could be the most exciting author-backed role. Om was signed on and plunged headlong into preparing for it.

The producers were Neo Films that comprised Manmohan Shetty, Pradeep Upoor and Shivanand Shetty, with whom Om formed a deep bond of

The hot-blooded conscientious policeman Om played in *Ardh Satya* caught the attention of millions of viewers in India and ensured Om's success in the film industry.

friendship over the years. For the first time Om joined a gym at the producers' expense at the Holiday Inn Hotel to tone up his otherwise lean frame.

Like a typical cop he also learnt to ride a motorbike. He was so thrilled when he learnt to ride it that he used to roam all over the city on his friend Ashok Banthia's bike. One day he drove up to Govind's house to impress him by driving him to Tardeo. Midway, the bike stopped. Om kick-started it and drove on. Further up near Century Bazaar, it stopped again. Om tried kick-starting it again. Govind was not impressed. An actor known to Govind happened to pass by so Govind took a lift from him and left Om to sort out the bike.

As a preparation for the role, Om also visited a couple of police stations, Mahim and Girgaum, to observe the behaviour of policemen when they were away from public scrutiny and to soak in the general ambience. One evening he was offered a drink called Maramari, which is half lemonade and half soda, so that the cops with their poor pay-packets get a taste of the fizz without having to pay for a full soda bottle. It was at the police station that he first heard about 'zero police', an unofficial police person, who sometimes doubles as a peon and an informer or *khabri*.

During the filming of *Ardh Satya* in Gamdevi, the policemen from the nearby police station came out and gaped at Naseer and Om, both in police uniform. 'But we are the real ones,' one of them said. Nevertheless, they were so impressed by the details and authenticity of the uniform that they asked for the name of the director.

Working in *Ardh Satya* was a fulfilling experience not only because of a good script and director but also because he had good co-stars. Smita Patil starred opposite him again after *Aakrosh*, apart from Naseer. And friend Amrish Puri – who most people mistake to be his real-life brother because of the similarity in their features and voice, besides their sharing a common surname – played his father.

An interesting incident transpired soon after the premiere of *Ardh Satya*. After the screening, Bauji was extremely upset with Om and very disturbed. The scene in the film between father and son was so universal that Bauji began to empathize with it. What was worse,

Govind Nihalani discussing the story with Om and Naseeruddin on the sets of *Droh Kaal*, nearly ten years after *Ardh Satya*.

Om's screen father, Amrish Puri slaps his screen mother. Bauji felt Om must have narrated his childhood experience to Govind which got played on screen. Little did he realize that it was Vijay Tendulkar's depiction of something that happens so commonly in the male-oriented Indian setup.

*Ardh Satya* went on to become not only a critically acclaimed film, but also did very well in the box office. It was the first time in Indian cinema that a so-called 'art film' with no songs or dances did this well commercially. The week the film was released, the famed Amitabh Bachchan-starrer, *Coolie*, was also running. Bachchan was already the reigning superstar by then but despite that *Ardh Satya* ran for twenty-two weeks, just short of the silver jubilee – that too because it was taken off the cinemas abruptly.

Om remembers the Friday the film was released. He drove down with Pradeep Upoor to the old Amber Oscar theatre in Irla (now Shoppers Stop). For an actor, it is one of the ultimate dreams to see himself on the hoardings. Om was '*maha* thrilled'. He was even more thrilled seeing people milling to get tickets and a 'Housefull' board dangling at the entrance. He was almost tempted to get down and wave at the crowds but restrained himself.

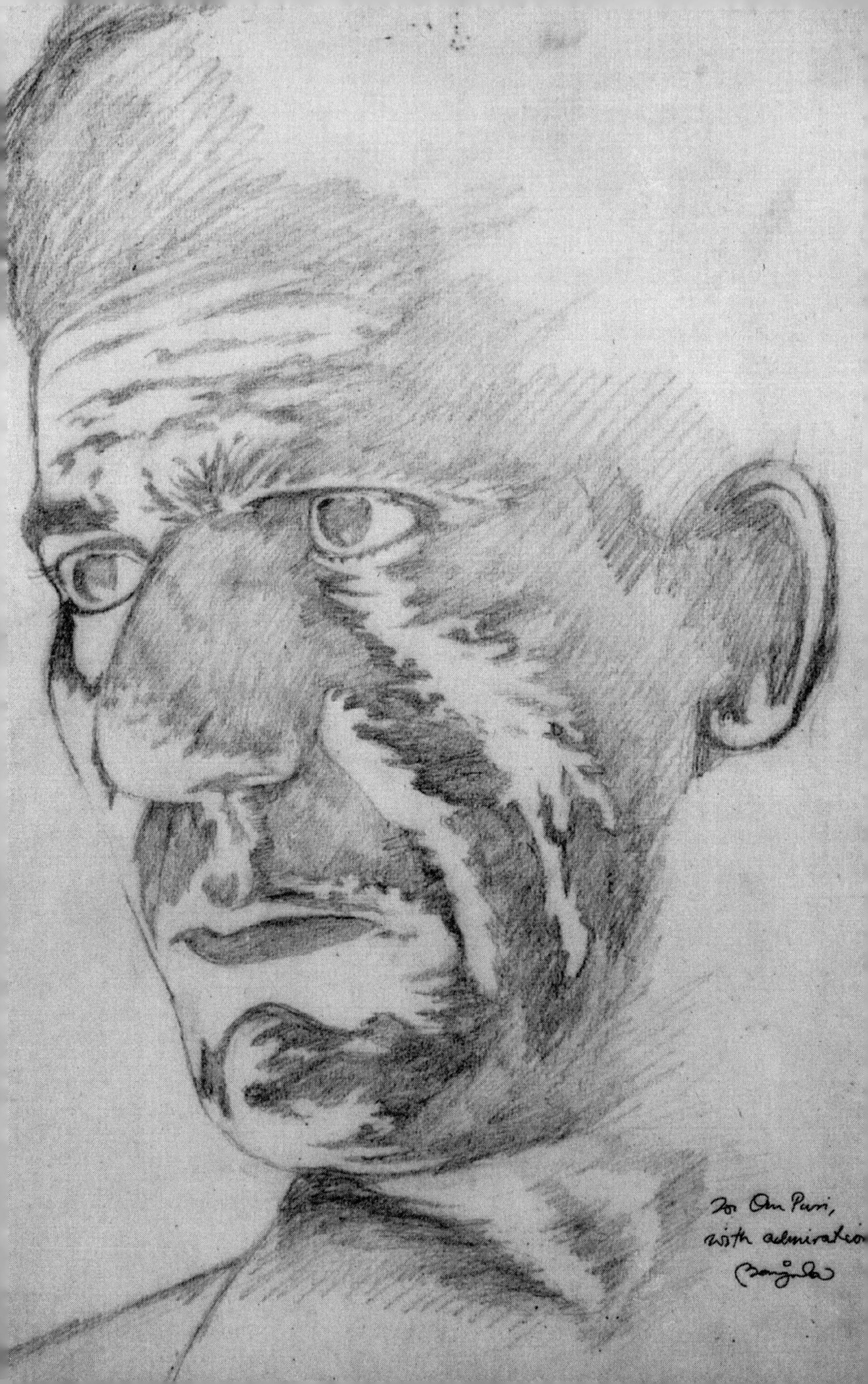
For Om Puri,
with admiratio

Ironically, when Govind first decided to film *Ardh Satya*, he had only one person in mind – the 'angry young man' of the day, Amitabh Bachchan. But Bachchan was busy fulfilling his big commercial ventures and had little time for a small-budget film, that too with a not-yet-famous filmmaker. Govind then approached Om. Again, ten years later, Govind's initial choice for the film *Droh Kaal* was Amitabh Bachchan but it did not work out. Finally, a decade after that in 2003, Govind realized his dream of working with Amitabh Bachchan in *Dev*. In *Dev*, he got both the celebrated actors from Indian cinema, one from the popular genre and one from the art genre, Amitabh Bachchan and Om Puri respectively, to work together for the first time.

One day during filming on the sets of *Dev*, Om caught Bachchan unawares. With a straight face he told him, 'Bachchan *saab*, I am eternally grateful to you.'

'Why?' Bachchan asked surprised.

'You have done me such a big favour.'

'Really?' Bachchan asked, even more puzzled. 'What is that?'

'I cannot thank you enough,' Om continued. The suspense was killing Bachchan and Om was secretly enjoying every moment of his bafflement.

'But what did I do? Tell me!' Bachchan asked impatiently.

'You refused to do *Ardh Satya*.'

'Did I?'

'Yes. You were too busy. Had you done the film I would have been nowhere today,' Om answered.

Amitabh Bachchan had a hearty laugh. 'I am glad I did. Because you did a much better job than I could have done. Incidentally, *Ardh Satya* is one of my favourite films.'

Bachchan said about Om's performance later: 'Despite his being physically not so commanding, his performance in *Ardh Satya* was physically arresting. Not forgetting his terrific voice.... Every actor enjoys a certain compatibility when the co-star is self-assured and does not step on your toes. That is the kind of comfort Om gives. Acting is all about reacting to the right performances with your colleagues. If a

Facing Page: A sketch done for the posters of *Ardh Satya* by acclaimed artist and writer, Manjula Padmanabhan; it carries the inscription 'For Om Puri, with admiration'.

sequence is right in *Dev*, the credit goes to Om. He is also perhaps one Indian actor who has been able to bridge Indian art cinema, Hindi commercial cinema and Western cinema.'

*Ardh Satya* remains one of the landmark films, not just for Amitabh Bachchan but for Indian cinema as a whole. It is a special favourite with the Indian police force and is shown in police training academies throughout the country. And police in the state of Maharashtra empathizes with the character of Anant Velanker the most.

With the release of *Ardh Satya*, Om tasted fame. 'For the first time commercial filmmakers woke up and took notice of me,' Om recollects. 'When soon after *Ardh Satya* I entered a studio one day, I felt people looking at me. I also walked with a slight attitude. Perhaps it was the first time stardom had hit me. Perhaps for the first time I felt like a celebrity.'

Apart from celebrity status, *Ardh Satya* also got him the National Award for Best Actor in 1984. He had earlier got the same award for Shyam Benegal's *Arohan*, which unfortunately did not get a theatre release except in West Bengal. Om's performance in *Ardh Satya*, however, was there for all to see.

*Ardh Satya* also got him his first major international award, at the Karlovy Vary Festival in Czechoslovakia, for the Best Actor. While most of his trophies and certificates are displayed at home, there is no keepsake from Karlovy Vary. The citation was lost by Govind Nihalani on the flight from Prague to Bombay. And a ceramic plaque was crashed to smithereens by me during one of our domestic quarrels!

Though the film was a milestone in his career and Om Puri now came to be known in film parlance as a 'bankable actor', *Ardh Satya* itself did not earn him much money. The first thing he did with part of the *Ardh Satya* booty was to buy a fridge and a small black-and-white television for Bauji to keep him entertained. Neighbours in the colony soon started befriending Bauji who was a very amiable fellow, albeit moody. Some of them would tell Bauji his son was doing very well and it was time they bought their own house.

'But Om has hardly earned from the film,' the old man would reply.

'That's what you think. He has stashed away all the cash safely somewhere. Either that or the producers are taking him for a ride,' they provoked him.

One day Bauji accosted Om as the latter entered the house. He sat on his son's chest, almost hitting him, asking him where he had kept the rest of the money. Om held his hand tightly, preventing the blow and warned Bauji never to take on him (much like the scene with Amrish Puri in his recent hit film!).

Though Om loved his father, father and son had their fair share of highs and lows.

Certain violent scenes of the film were written and executed so powerfully that they are counted among Om's most notable performances in his entire career.

# An Actor at Last

*Ardh Satya* made life as an actor easier for Om. Film offers started pouring in; though this did not mean that money poured in as well. But things became much easier financially. He was assured of constant work and now, at the age of thirty-four, he could happily call himself a full-time 'film actor'. He did not have to depend on other means of livelihood like working in an office, doing theatre or teaching. The goal he had set out to achieve when he had left Patiala in 1970 was at last realized after almost fifteen years.

Om worked under a gamut of interesting and talented film directors and with many notable artists. This phase of socially relevant, meaningful cinema continued for almost a decade, till the nineties with Goutam Ghose's *Patang* (1994) and Prakash Jha's *Mrityudand* (1997).

Not only meaningful cinema, the eighties was also a period of meaningful television. Television had come to India around the mid-seventies. For many years since its inception, it was ruled by the single government-run channel, Doordarshan. Being a new and accessible medium, some of the finest filmmakers of the period decided to delve into this relatively unknown sphere.

Om was fortunate to be part of some of the best works that Indian television has ever seen. He was part of Shyam Benegal's *Yatra*, Indian Railways' tribute to India, and *Bharat Ek Khoj*; Basu Chatterjee's *Kakaji Kahin*; Ketan Mehta's *Mr Yogi*; Sai Paranjpe's *Sparsh*; Gulzar's *Kirdar*; and not to forget Govind Nihalani's magnum opus for television, *Tamas*.

Facing page: Om's talent got him prestigious assignments, including international ones, like Roland Joffe's *City of Joy*, where he played to perfection the role of a rickshaw-puller in Kolkata.

After *Kirdar*, Gulzar said, 'He is a seamless actor. I have never seen him act, even in the most dramatic scenes. He gets so much into the skin of a character.... When I first saw *Sparsh*, I was bowled by Naseer's performance ... But after seeing Om's small role, I thought he was the cherry-topping in the film.'

One of the remarkable aspects of his acting was pointed out by Satyajit Ray's son, filmmaker Sandip Ray: 'Another great quality which I observed in him (during my film *Target*) and which for an actor is very essential is that he does not blink! When I asked him he told me he could hold on for any length of time without blinking.'

As for Shyam Benegal's opinion, 'Whenever I think of *Bharat Ek Khoj*, I think of Om Puri. One of the most complex characters he played was that of Duryodhan where he had to give a nine-minute speech. That showed his ability and stamina.... To me what is commendable about Om is that he made possible what was impossible. With his unorthodox looks in an industry that thrives on good looks, he made it possible as an actor. And that, according to me, is his highest accolade.'

In between Indian films and television, Om managed a cameo in Richard Attenborough's *Gandhi* in 1985, his first small foray into international cinema. 'We needed an actor who could underplay the role and make the scene less theatrical, less filmy. This was in a way the signifying climax of the film as it was nearing its end. I am unequivocal in my admiration for Om's underplaying the role. As an actor he was superb.... Om Puri is a superb and distinguished actor of the highest calibre,' recollects Lord Attenborough.

Whilst his co-star, Sir Ben Kingsley, had this to offer: 'My recollections of working with Om are absolutely indelible. His bursting into Gandhiji's fast, demanding, "Bapu eat," is the hinge point of the film – so often cited as a remarkable clip. Om's passionate commitment to his character's grief and rage is profoundly moving. He becomes emblematic of all who suffered terribly during Partition. It was my great fortune to work with such a great and unique actor.'

Soon after *Ardh Satya*, Om expressed his desire to buy his own place to Manmohan Shetty, who told him to go right ahead.

Om receives the Soviet Land Nehru Award in 1986.

'But I don't have enough money,' Om told him.

'Doesn't matter. We will loan you the amount,' he said reassuringly, including Pradeep Upoor in the offer.

'But it is a huge amount and I don't have a guarantor,' Om argued.

'Well, you yourself are the guarantor. After *Ardh Satya*, you will have no problem getting work. You can return the loan then,' Shetty replied.

And sure enough, Om was able to pay back the loan within a year. The first piece of property Om bought in Bombay was situated in Versova, which was mainly a marshland in the mid-eighties but is one of the most stylish suburbs today. It is the last of the seven islands that make up the city of Bombay, starting with Colaba in the extreme south and ending with Versova in the north. Om zeroed in on a 'two-bedroom-hall-kitchen flat', as it is referred to in Bombay parlance, situated on the top floor of a seven-storey apartment building, Trishul, in a palm-lined stretch called Seven Bunglows. Local stories go that Seven Bunglows originally comprised seven huge bungalows owned by seven Parsi sisters.

Om had always wanted a bit of the open sky in his house and was ecstatic when he found this place. The apartment looked out onto the

Arabian Sea and up to Madh Island on one side, while the other side had a terrace overlooking verdant greenery. Not in his wildest dreams, while shifting from one rented room to another, had Om imagined he would one day own a small place in Bombay that was virtually a penthouse. And for the next twenty-five years, the apartment in Trishul was to be his 'home' in the megacity, seeing him through good days and lean days, happy days and sad days.

While the building was still under construction, Shetty offered Om his Chembur apartment for the interim period. The Bhagat Singh Colony room had become too cramped for the rising star. By now he had another girlfriend, Mala, who had done her master's in Indian classical music and had come from Benaras to make her career in Bombay. When Om shifted to Chembur, Mala moved in with him and Bauji. Thus, she became his girlfriend 'officially' and they began to be known as a couple in their circle.

When the three of them finally shifted to Trishul, in true filmy style Om acquired the services of a secretary, one Mr Satya Prakash Dubey, known to all as Dubeyji. Dubeyji's contribution far exceeded that of a regular secretary. Keeping Om's dates and collecting his fees was just one part of the job. He also bought the weekly ration, paid the bills, ordered the gas, fixed the car and conducted small repair works at home. Dubeyji would be with Om for the next twelve years or so, serving as agent, friend, manager, accountant, all rolled into one.

Besides Dubeyji, Om also hired a regular make-up man, Vijay Sawant, who has been with him for nearly twenty-five years now. Vijay is the son of Ramchandra Sawant, generally known as 'Dada', who was the make-up man to top stars, including Rekha. Vijay has also served an assortment of top actors but is generally known as Om Puri's makeup man in the industry. With Vijay, who has a mischievous sense of humour and is constantly up to pranks, Om shares an easygoing relationship. The most notable quality in him, in Om's words, is that 'in spite of our closeness, he has never once stepped beyond his limits. Sometimes, my other staff has crossed their limits with me. Never Vijay.'

After Dubeyji, the new man on the horizon was Sunil Gaur, who had worked for Lata Mangeshkar and Gulzar. While Dubeyji was

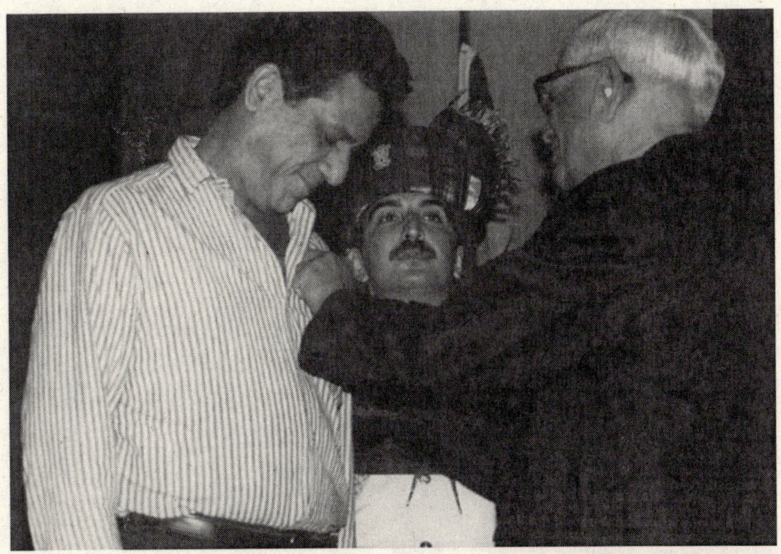

The Padma Shri presented by President R. Venkatraman to Om at the Rashtrapati Bhawan in New Delhi in 1990.

voluble, Sunil belies the typical Bollywood manager – he is extremely soft-spoken and calm, a perfect foil to Om's booming outbursts. Over the years, Sunil Gaur has turned out to be more than a professional colleague. He is a friend, but like Vijay, he remains gently unobtrusive. It was also partly Sunil's initiative to steer Om gradually from small-budget films to bigger banners. Today, Om has become an integral part of David Dhawan's, Priyadarshan's and Vipul Shah's units.

In the popular film industry, stars love being followed by their entourage that often includes a secretary or manager, a publicist, a makeup man, a hair dresser, a costume designer, a driver and even a spot boy who serves tea and holds the umbrella. In contrast, Om's entourage for years has consisted only of Dubeyji and Vijay. While Vijay kept him company on his long shoots, it was Dubeyji who held fort at home in Bombay, and after him, Sunil Gaur.

It was with Trishul that Om at last gave Bauji the security of having a roof over his head. Bauji had his own room but loved going about visiting friends, mainly Om's. Many a time he made Om's friends uncomfortable by calling on them at odd hours but they accommodated Bauji as they would a little child.

Om had a special relationship with his father, or Bauji, who could be whimsical and mischievous even with Om's friends.

Bauji would also try and mould Om in little ways. His biggest grouse with Om was why the latter did not settle down and have children. Bauji loved and indulged the neighbours' children often. But Om was happy with his bachelor status and was least interested in being tied down by marriage. Bauji of course could neither fathom this, nor why Mala did not pursue Om.

Once on the sets of *Shrant*, Bauji liked the actress Geeta Khanna, who was playing Om's screen wife. There was a husband-wife photograph of them on the sets that Bauji liked the look of. He even found out that she had her own apartment in Santa Cruz. Wasting no time, Bauji approached her parents with a proposal without Om's knowledge. When Om learnt about it, he was angry at and embarrassed by Bauji.

'But I thought it would be good for you. Besides, she has her own house,' Bauji replied like a simpleton.

One day Bauji called up Om's friend, actor Tom Alter.

'What is it Bauji?' Tom asked.

'I am alone. I need to talk to you,' Bauji sounded disturbed.

Knowing Om was not in town, Tom was worried and drove down from Pedder Road all the way to Versova, a good hour-long drive to find out what was bothering the old man.

'Tell your friend to get married,' Bauji told Tom when he arrived.

'Is this why you called me all the way? To tell me this. You could have said it over the phone!' Tom was justifiably harassed. But at the same time Bauji's naïve concern for Om increased Tom's fondness for the old man.

Om drinking and having a chat with the doyen among lyricists of Hindi cinema, Gulzar, in 1997.

Once Bauji refused to let Om and his friend Ashok Banthia enter the house as both of them had gone out for a party and were a little late in returning.

'But you cannot lock us out the whole night,' Om yelled.

'Why not?' Bauji yelled back from across the door.

'Because it is Ashok's house you are in,' Om replied, embarrassed. But Bauji was adamant. Om and Ashok had to go to Dubeyji's cramped apartment to spend the night.

But one of the most memorable incidents with Bauji happened at the Prithvi Theatre where Naseer and Benjamin Gilani were performing *Waiting for Godot*. Om was away. Bauji decided to take a friend from Punjab who wanted to see a play in the famed Prithvi Theatre. When they reached, the play had started and tickets were all sold out.

'Never mind, just follow me. Everyone knows me here,' Bauji told the man as he tried to impress him by taking him from the backstage. They both entered the main hall but since it was dark and there were no seats empty nearby, Bauji motioned the man to just sit where they were. Naseer and Benji were performing and they suddenly froze midway into their act when they saw two men crossing the stage.

The audience was also baffled and wondered whether Godot had finally arrived! Seconds later, the actors realized it was Om's father, and some members from the audience also recognized him. After a moment's hesitation, the actors continued with the play whilst some murmurs from the audience were heard repeating, 'Hey, its Om's father, Om's father.'

After the play, Bauji had the audacity to introduce the gentleman to Naseer. When asked later, Naseer says his first reaction was anger, then sheer amusement. 'Bauji nearly f****d up my play!'

That was Bauji. At times naïve. At times irritating. There are so many such incidents that one can write a book on Bauji's idiosyncrasies alone. Om's relation with Bauji was tumultuous, both sharing an underlying bond of love, peppered with heated arguments and quarrels.

❧

Around that time, Om decided to do something more for his family than just supporting them financially. During one of his rare visits to his brother's in Ludhiana, Om realized that Ved was not the hardworking sort. Nor did he have enough enterprise. Om had invested in a 'tent hire' business for Ved but when Dubeyji had a look at the accounts, they saw that the business was running at a complete loss. Om told his brother to fold the business up and assured that he would continue to support him.

As brothers, Om and Ved shared a cordial relationship although temperamentally, both were diametrically opposite. Ved was a quiet, soft-spoken man and some people even found Ved unsocial as he mostly grunted in monosyllables. While Om seemed to have inherited Bauji's fiery temper, Ved Puri was so mild that one never even saw him 'shoo' a fly away. As a child, Ved also used to get beaten up by Bauji but unlike Om, he was too meek to rebel. The only time Ved showed his temper was when he and Om were having a heated argument, and Ved, unable to match Om's vocal strength, just banged the door loudly and left the house.

Om and his nephews and nieces with Shashi Kapoor and Rajiv Kapoor. From left to right: The boys are Yash (or Rinku), Vicky and Bobby and the girls are Divya and Saumya, Raghukul Chaddha's daughters.

Knowing Ved's lackadaisical attitude, Ved's wife had to be more enterprising of the two. But she would constantly complain about money. Om also noticed that Ved's four boys were not doing much in life. They did not attend school regularly and were just wasting away at home. 'They would play in the *mohalla* with running noses and black fingernails,' Om remembers. 'At first I was shocked to see them. Their teeth were yellowed and I had to teach them basic hygiene like brushing their teeth regularly and cleaning themselves properly. It was then that I felt I should bring them to Bombay and provide them with better education – maybe they would wake up and do something with their lives.'

In 1986 Om sent his nephews to a boarding school in Udaipur. The boys did not fare well academically so he finally brought them with him to Bombay.

The two older boys were not interested in studies; Bobby dropped out in eighth standard and Vicky followed him soon. The third in line, Rinku, was a little more studious. So Om used his contacts and

got him admission in Wilson College. Unfortunately, Rinku got into wrong company and soon left college.

Om was heartbroken. It appeared like all his efforts had failed. He did not know who to blame. One day he called the boys and explained to them that even if they did not enjoy studies, they could pursue any professional course or career they were interested in. And they should give their best to it. After much dallying, Bobby decided to become a chef, while Vicky got admitted in the two-year training programme at the Oberoi group of hotels. Today, Vicky is married with a daughter and manages a resort near Pune.

Bobby's first job as a trainee chef began with the Horizon Hotel in Juhu (now defunct). When he came home after his first day at work, Om asked him how it was. 'Uncle, today I just defeathered hundred chickens,' Bobby said, sounding completely drained. For many years, Bobby worked as a chef in Pune's Shantai Hotel. Despite his promising potential as a cook, Bobby quit his job as a chef to try easy ways to wealth. After trying his hand at real estate and having a brush with the law, he is today professionally still undecided. He lives in Pune with his son and wife, who ironically, is a postgraduate.

Once again Rinku had professed interest to resume his studies and tried to complete graduation privately but soon after decided to join films, though he was unsure in what capacity. Om sent Rinku to Pradeep Upoor, who was now producing television serials, to train as a lab assistant. From a lab assistant, Rinku graduated to editing some of the popular TV serials of the day. Rinku is also married and settled in Bombay with two children. The youngest nephew, Rocky, the most serious and sincere of the lot is working as a chef in one of Bombay's exclusive restaurants, Indigo.

There was a time when seeing their wild ways, Om had felt completely frustrated as a guardian. 'But today I feel happy to see them well-settled and I know I have rehabilitated an entire family. I consider that a contribution to society,' says the proud uncle.

Facing page: Om in Russia in 1987. This ten-day tour was offered to him for winning the Soviet Land Nehru award.

Posters of the movies Om did with international stars; and a still from Rajkumar Santoshi's *China Gate*.

# Let's Go to the Movies

In a career spanning over three decades with more than two hundred odd films, it becomes difficult to talk in detail about the actor's experiences with every filmmaker and the entire cast. There were even times when Om couldn't remember a film and was even pleasantly surprised, when he saw himself in an old film being screened on television. But there are some films that are very important to an actor in terms of experience as well as success. Here, we talk about some of them.

### Arohan

*Arohan* was one of Shyam Benegal's first films in which Om essayed the lead role of Hari Mondal, a farmer who is wronged by the landlord. In order to get into the skin of the character, Om would sit in the sun, oiled and bare-bodied to get the right tan and walked with a limp throughout the film. The film was shot near Bolpur near Tagore's Santiniketan. It got him his first National Award for Best Actor, though it never had a theatre release besides in West Bengal and Bihar.

Om calls Shyam *babu* his walking encyclopaedia. He has a faultless sense of history. A pioneer of New Wave cinema, Benegal had a hand in reviving the socially relevant films of Guru Dutt, Bimal Roy, V. Shantaram and others. And yet Om has never found him arrogant or boastful.

### Bharat Ek Khoj

*Bharat Ek Khoj* or *Discovery of India* was based on the eponymous book by Jawaharlal Nehru, running over fifty-two episodes where Om played more than fifteen different characters, besides doing the voice-over for all the episodes. It was a very strenuous experience for a year when Om would leave home at eight in the morning for Film City, return not before ten at night, shower, do his lines for next day, have dinner, sleep and start over again the next morning. He only had Sundays off. The lines were not easy and there were long passages to memorize.

To him, *Discovery* was one very satisfying project. It was a well-researched serial and portrayed the history of the country from a secular and unbiased perspective. Though it

A scene from Shyam Benegal's televised serial, *Bharat Ek Khoj*.

was shown on television many years ago, it should be shown continuously in a loop. DVDs and CDs should be made available easily to school students and shown as part of the curriculum.

**Bhavni Bhavai**

*Bhavni Bhavai*, was a good film about the old tale of untouchables and was one of the reasons for Om's doing it. Though made in Gujarati, had all non-Gujarati actors. It was a major task working on the cast's Gujarati dialogues everyday. The film was shot in a little village called Vaso, near Ahmedabad.

Om enjoyed working with Ketan Mehta, the director who was always willing to experiment with different genres of filmmaking. For his pint-sized frame, his films are ironically made on large canvasses.

Smita was already a star when Om first worked with her but her warmth made him feel at ease. She was a very fine human being, a genuinely friendly person. Her personality reflected on the screen as well and unlike a number of others, she was never crafty. As an actress she was instinctive, just like her bohemian, *bindaas* self. Om shared an easy on-screen relation with her.

He used to visit her home in Tardeo and still remembers she used to serve him tea and buttered toasts. The toasts, especially, were unique and delicious. Once curiosity got the better of Om and he asked her how she made them.

'Simple. Just butter the bread and put it in the toaster. That's all.'

'Smita Patil toasts' are made in our house to this date.

## Chand Pardesi

*Chand Pardesi* was a social film with a rural background and was shot in villages outside of Patiala. In the film Om plays a munshi to Amrish Puri, the landlord. It was a landmark film in Punjabi cinema. It was the first time Punjabi middle-class and upper middle-class audience went to the theatre to watch a film. Produced in 1981 by some of Om's theatre films friends from Patiala like Yograj Chedda, J.S. Cheema and Baldev Gill, the film was directed by another young and talented filmmaker, Chitrarth. Even till date it remains a landmark film in Punjab and people still remember his dialogues.

## Chachi 420

If ever Om has sent a fan letter to a colleague it was to southern superstar, Kamal Hasan. Once, Om bumped into him on a flight. Their eyes met and Kamal asked, 'Am I right?' Om was flattered and said, 'Yes.'

Soon after, Om sent him a letter after watching *Nayakan*. Years later, when Om was working with him in *Chachi 420*, he asked him whether he had received the letter at all. Kamal nodded.

'Then why did you not reply?'

'I was too embarrassed,' Kamal said.

For years Om had been looking for an opportunity to work with him. So, when Kamal Hasan sent Om the Tamil script of *Chachi 420*, Om was not as excited about the role as about the prospect of working with Kamal Hasan. And after that film his friendship with Kamal blossomed.

Kamal is a disciplined actor and like Robert de Niro, prepares conscientiously for his roles – even gaining or losing weight as the role demands. He thinks ahead of his time and is an unconventional filmmaker. He is a gambler and is willing to stake everything for his creativity. As a producer he is very generous and as a director, very patient with his actors and also extremely cool.

## Charlie Wilson's War

Almost thirteen years after *Wolf*, Mike Nichols, who is very fond of Om, requested his agent Jeremy to cast Om in his film *Charlie Wilson's War* as former Pakistani president, General Zia-ul-Haq. It was a cameo and initially Om was a bit hesitant but I assured him the script was fine. Then Mike Nichols called him up and admonished him like one does an erring child. Om took it on and was extremely happy with the decision, especially as he immediately struck a chord with the lead actor Tom Hanks.

Though a huge star and currently one of the highest paid actors in the world, Tom is full of fun. He is always joking around on the sets and dissolving serious moments into

With the stars of *China Gate* (L to R Kulbhushan Kharbanda, Sameer Soni, Om, Danny Denzongpa, Amrish Puri and Viju Khote).

laughter. He is extremely relaxed and not patronizing. His eyes are always shining like a child's. But when it comes to performing, he is dead serious. As an actor, he isn't status conscious despite his large entourage.

Once Ishaan and I had come to the sets and Om asked him if he could spare five minutes for us. 'Why five? Let us have a meal together.' Later that evening, we all went out for dinner and he did not bring anyone else along. It was a pleasant evening with Tom sharing stories of his family and a pizza with Ishaan.

**China Gate**

*China Gate* was a very important film in Om's career, where he played the lead in a commercial film for the first time. The story revolved around seven ex-army men who try and rescue a village from a dreaded dacoit gang. But the filmmaker, Rajkumar Santoshi was indulgent, overshot and went overboard. The team went to Hampi nearly five times and the film took forever to complete. There was even a fifteen-day period of re-shoot, which is totally unlike Govind Nihalani, Raj's mentor. The final outcome of the film was not up to the expectations. Yet, Raj is a filmmaker to reckon with in commercial cinema. Even though his films are more commercial than Prakash Jha's, he knows his craft well.

Raj's other weakness is chicken and he overindulges in that too. Once he came home for an impromptu meal and got a four-tiered tiffin carrier. When I opened it, it contained chicken,

With long-time friend and co-actor of Roland Joffe's *City of Joy*, Patrick Swayze.

chicken and more chicken cooked in a variety of styles. Om joked with Raj that the only thing left is to cook a chicken dessert for him!

**City of Joy**

Roland Joffe's *City of Joy* was Om's first major role in an international project. Based on Dominique Lapierre's eponymous award-winning novel, this was his big break in Hollywood. He essayed the role of Hasari Pal, the rickshaw-puller, one of the two lead characters. The film was shot over three months in Calcutta and a few scenes were done in London's Pinewood Studio.

Roland Joffe as a director was very strict and stubborn but he is an exceptionally focussed person. He knows exactly what he wants and refuses to budge. Despite his recalcitrance, he is disciplined and working with him was Om's first exposure to working on a truly large international canvas.

Om was in awe of Patrick Swayze and a bit nervous when he first learnt Patrick would be his co-actor. This was to be Om's first interaction with a big Hollywood star. But Patrick Swayze turned out to be a big surprise. Fresh from his stardom, Patrick was the epitome of humility and friendliness. He was a practising Buddhist and believed in some Eastern philosophies. According to him, Om reminded him of his father. 'You intimidate me,' he had said on his first meeting with him. Om never asked him why.

Though Patrick and Om rarely met, they shared deep love and respect for each other. When Om got the news of Patrick's demise he was devastated but

With Deepa Mehta, who was eager to have Om in her directorial debut, *Sam & Me*.

not shocked as he knew it was coming. So many images of Patrick and him from his first day in Calcutta to their trips in Japan and Australia flashed by. Om felt sad because he lost him too early – at 57 rather than the other way around, at 75. He was gentle and kind and a fabulous dancer. Om misses him dearly.

Om always prepares for the role he plays in each film, but *City of Joy* was special. He started preparing well in advance. He started learning to pull a rickshaw from two regular rickshaw-pullers. They would start out early in the morning and return to the hotel before the traffic started. After a few days, Om realized that most of the rickshaw-pullers ran barefoot. The first few days were tough but slowly, he managed.

There are a number of memorable anecdotes connected with the shooting. Om recalls once he stopped at a roadside tea-stall to have a cup of tea. It was early morning and two elderly customers were drinking tea there. On seeing Om, one of them remarked to the other, '*Arrey*, doesn't this rickshaw fellow remind you of Om Puri?' To which the other nodded. 'Such similar features!' he exclaimed.

When Om finished his tea, he told them that he was indeed Om Puri. They looked at him, not quite believing him or their eyes. Later, as he was leaving, he heard the tea-stall owner exclaiming, '*Bechara*. Poor man. How sad to see him reduced to this state. He used to be such a fine actor. And imagine him pulling a rickshaw now? Must have fallen on real hard days.' At this Om could not help smiling to himself. His hard work had paid off.

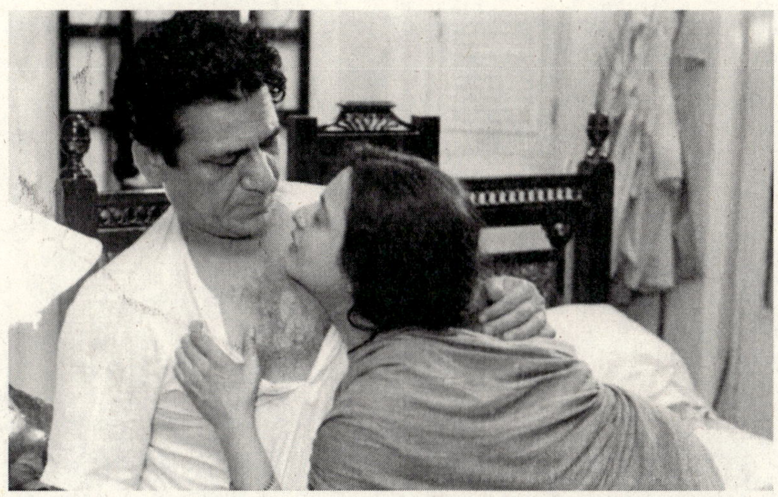

With co-star Rekha in Basu Bhattacharya's sizzling yet poignant film, *Aastha*.

Om had a lot of hopes and aspirations pinned to this film and he gave his very best. Unfortunately, the film did not do well, though his performance was noticed. *The New York Times* reviewer wrote, 'Puri's performance will make you cry.' Patrick Swayze had also remarked at a press conference in Australia that 'if anyone deserves an Oscar this year, it is Om'. Though Om has never really performed for awards, it was this once that he expected at least an Oscar nomination. For once he dreamt of having a parallel career in films outside India but it was not to be. However, Om did get noticed reasonably well in the US post *City of Joy*.

Once, a couple of years later, Om and I were having coffee in Columbia University campus, when a couple of students came up to Om and lauded his performance in the film. It was touching to be thus remembered, Om feels.

**Dharavi**

*Dharavi*, based on Asia's largest slum, is a Sudhir Mishra film. Sudhir is very sure of his craft, and though he may not be that organized, he is flexible as a director. The film was an eye-opener for Om as he learnt so much about the place that has several small-scale industries within its precincts. It is a world on its own. It was also the first film where Om worked with the 'dreamgirl' of those times, Madhuri Dixit. Om found her to be an extremely disciplined actress, who had her head on her shoulders despite her reigning stardom. To Om, Madhuri epitomizes the ideal middle-class success story of hard work combined with the requisite pinch of luck.

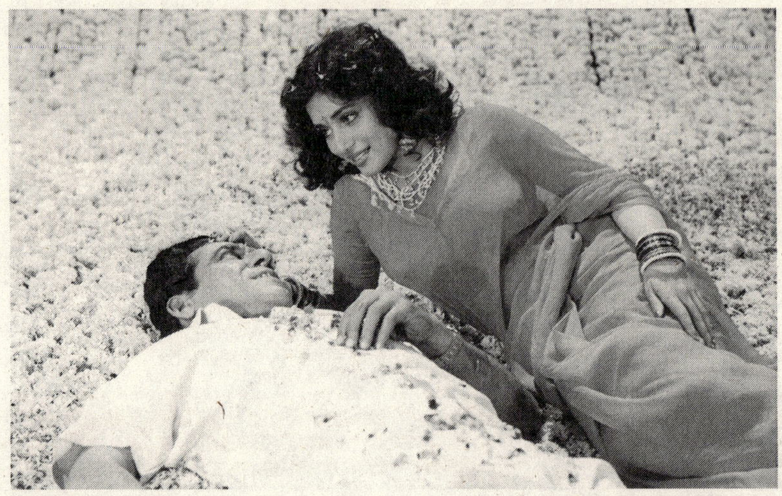

With Madhuri Dixit in *Dharavi*.

**East is East**

*East is East* is based on the successful West End play, written by Ayub Khan-Din, which is semi-autobiographical. First they had approached Om for the play which he declined as he could not spare that many days. But when the film was offered, Om accepted. He plays the UK-settled Pakistani patriarch George Khan, who is married to an Irish woman and is a bit of a Hitler to his family.

The director, Damien O'Donnell is an extremely talented director and has a childlike honesty. At the outset he had told Om, 'I am not very familiar with Eastern culture, so please don't hesitate to point out my mistakes.' No one could have said this was Damien's first film. Om feels Damien is single-handedly responsible for making him a household name in the UK.

A week before filming, Damien had organized a workshop with the actors. A day before the shoot Om realized he was speaking Indian-accented English. He wondered how to tackle it since it was too late for him to cultivate a British accent. It then dawned on him that having been married to and living with an Irish woman for twenty years, he would automatically pick up his English from her. So Om made Linda Bassett (who plays his wife) read his lines and he underlined the words with the accent.

Linda is a great human being and a great actress. It was unbelievable that *East is East* was her first film. Her confidence in front of the camera was astonishing, especially as Linda is extremely gentle and modest.

A few days before the shoot, Om called his 'entire family' in the film to our apartment in Holland Park for a meal as part of a bonding exercise.

With Shabana Azmi in *City of Joy* where she played Hasari Pal's wife, Kamla.

Some of the children brought a home-cooked item each and we all cooked together. Damien joined us at midnight with a bottle of champagne. This helped us connect as a family throughout the film.

After the film was over the unit had a wrap-up party as is the custom. But this one was different from the others. Om and I had to leave a little early as we had an early-morning flight to catch. His entire 'Khan family' came out to bid us goodbye. As we got into the car and the driver started to drive, they ran behind it, all the way up to the gates of Ealing Studios. It was very touching.

**Gandhi**

Directed by Richard Attenborough, *Gandhi* was a very prestigious project for Om. He was lucky to work with Sir Ben Kingsley in his short appearance in the film. A trained and versatile actor, Ben excels in every role and was brilliant as the Mahatma in the film. The proudest moment for Om was when that single scene he had done with Ben was shown at the Oscars.

**Hera Pheri**

*Hera Pheri* is one of the most successful comic flicks made in recent times by Priyadarshan. It is a situational comedy like most of his recent films. *Hera Pheri* was a pioneer in this genre and Priyan created his loyal team with Paresh Rawal, who is brilliant, and Akshay Kumar, who is a star today.

Priyadarshan started out with serious films like *Kala Pani, Virasat* and such others but since the past few years, Om rags him that he has opened up a 'comedy shop'. He is a prolific filmmaker, averaging a minimum of

With co-actor Smita Patil in *Sadgati*.

four films a year. He is well-versed in his craft and perhaps the only filmmaker who does not take lengthy shots. He lets his cameraman do the general lighting and then he shoots fast. Om loves working with him as he does not believe in night shoots. For him, a day can stretch maximum up to 9.30 p.m.

He is perhaps the only director who has directed more than a hundred films. He works non-stop, back to back, and Om joked with him once that was he ever to pen his autobiography, he should call it *Non-Stop*!

**In Custody**

*In Custody*, based on a novel by Anita Desai, was Ismail Merchant's debut film as a director. The film was shot in Bhopal and Om says he enjoyed working with the unit. Ismail was fun to be with, full of charm, exuberance and *joie de vivre*.

But Om, however, cannot say much for his directorial skills. He was quite impatient as a director and having worked as a producer for years he had a producer's hangover while directing. Once during a scene, a goat sauntered into the shot and Ismail ran behind it to chase it out. He had to be reminded that it was no longer his job to do that!

More than a filmmaker, he was a great person to be with. For instance, after the shoot for *Wolf*, Om and I went to his country house by the Hudson. Ruth Prawar Jhabwala was also there and Ismail and Om cooked a couple of delightful dishes. Ismail loved to announce his cooking with a great flourish. Once, Ruth asked him, 'What is this? Mmm, it's delicious.'

Satyajit Ray with his eye on the camera directs Om and Smita Patil in *Sadgati*.

Ismail replied, 'Ah! That my dear is lentil dumplings in a little sweet yoghurt tempered with cumin seeds and red chilly powder.'

'*Arrey*, it is simple *dahi-vada*,' Om exclaimed after tasting it, puncturing Ismail's pomposity at one go. Those were wonderful times and it is still hard to believe he is no more.

**Jaane Bhi Do Yaaro**

*Jaane Bhi Do Yaaro* went on to become a cult film. Kundan is a bit of a scatterbrain and looks a little lost on the sets. He exudes a kind of nervous energy. But the nice thing about him is that he trusts the actors and lets them improvize. He does not go strictly by the rule books.

The film was made on an extremely low budget, so low that the food came from Kundan's house! His wife cooked with the help of two *bais* (maids) and Om remembers there would be *dhudhi* (gourd) curry and *alu sabzi* (potatoes) almost everyday. He rarely wanted to break for lunch as time was money, and if he did, he would pick up the plate while the last shot was being taken and after announcing 'Action', he would start filling up his plate. By the time he said 'Cut', he would start eating. While the shot was being canned he would urge others, 'Hurry up. Eat fast,' as he had already eaten and was ready to shoot.

Since they could not afford a hotel and the shoot was in Alibaug, actors would take turns sleeping on the verandah of the shooting bungalow, literally on the floor. The crew members were not so lucky as they had to shoot virtually without a break, day and night. Once the DOP, Vinod Pradhan,

From L to R: Om in one of the many roles he played in Benegal's *Bharat Ek Khoj*; Metro cinema hall in Kolkata advertising film *Aakrosh* as a 'winner' as it ran to packed houses for many weeks.

was found sleeping in an upright position with his eye on the camera! The unit realized it when no sound came from the camera after the director announced, 'Roll Camera'. It was the poorest film unit Om worked with but it was loads of fun. And that goes on to prove that simply having great sets and locations, with a lot of glitter does not necessarily make an everlasting film.

**Kakaji Kahin**

*Kakaji Kahin*, a political satire for television was one of Basu Chatterjee's acclaimed works for Indian television, based on a book called *Netaji Kahin* by Manohar Shyam Joshi. Loosely translated, it means 'Where is Kakaji?' Om played the lead character of an aspiring and corrupt power broker with a great sense of humour.

Basuda was an economic film-maker but he was a little casual. He used a lot of zoom and compromised cleverly on locations – not a very smart thing to do in film grammar. He is one director, who if he tells you he requires you till say, 3 p.m., chances are he will release you by 1 p.m. Once when a location was not available, he shot the remaining bit by taking close-ups of the actor against a black background!

**Maachis**

Om has been an admirer of Gulzar *saab's* work and was thrilled when he first asked him to work in his television serial called *Kirdar*. Gulzar *saab* follows the Bimal Roy school of cinema and is known for his penchant

A scene from *Aarohan* with Victor Banerjee.

for adapting and being inspired by great books and films. He is always encouraging youngsters and newcomers and constantly eggs them on to do well. One of his greatest gifts to the film industry is music director and filmmaker, Vishal Bharadwaj.

The much acclaimed film, *Maachis*, was inspired by a small incident during the Tsar's regime in Russia in which Gulzar *saab* saw parity with Punjab terrorism. It was amazing that such a small emotion could inspire a whole train of ideas resulting in a feature.

**Mandi**

*Mandi* by Shyam Benegal was a great experience as Om had a long stint outdoors and stayed in the charming city of Hyderabad. It also had the stars of art cinema and it felt like one big family. In fact, Shyam *babu* always treated his unit like a family. He loved playing the benevolent patriarch. The high point would be sharing a peg or two with Shyam *babu* every evening and having sensible conversations.

In *Mandi* Om worked with Shabana Azmi for the first time, after which they did many films together where she played opposite Om. Shabana is a great actress, extremely professional and meticulous. She can sometimes go to the extent of participating in the script if her character is not well-rounded but she is also quite protective of newcomers and younger co-stars.

**Maqbool**

*Maqbool* is based on Shakespeare's *Macbeth* but adapted brilliantly to reflect the Indian social milieu by the writer Abbas Tyrewala. For example,

Om as the Pakistani cab driver in *My Son the Fanatic* by Hanif Kureishi.

the witches of Shakespeare's age are depicted as the corrupt police officials of today.

The director, Vishal Bharadwaj is a big surprise for the film industry. First, he surprised everyone with his innovative music in *Maachis*, and then, of course, with his directorial skills in *Maqbool*, and with other films. He is a very significant director and Om sees his contribution increasing in the years to come. He is extremely unassuming on the sets though he has a sharp eye for details.

As colleagues, Naseer and Om complement each other with ease. The filming of the two cops in this movie went off so effortlessly, joking and pulling each other's legs that they didn't even realize when the film shoot was over.

Naseer is an extremely intelligent actor. He is well-read and researches his roles well. Some of his films that Om particularly likes are *Paar*, *Sparsh*, and the recent *Shoot on Sight* – in all of which Naseer has been absolutely brilliant. They share one of the greatest friendships in the Hindi film industry, though it has never been conventional. Their has been a blow-hot-blow-cold relation over many years. But despite their disagreements, their grudging admiration for each other has survived.

**My Son the Fanatic**

In 1996, Om shot for his first major British film, *My Son the Fanatic*, where he plays a Pakistani cab driver. Written by Hanif Kureishi, it is very relevant to the subject of religious (in)tolerance. The director, Udayan Prasad's initial choice was Naseer because of the anti-

In yet another role as a Pakistani, with Linda Bassett as his Irish wife, in *East is East.*

Muslim sentiments examined in the film, but Naseer declined. That is when Om came in.

The character of Pervez is of a true world-citizen on account of his mindset. Pervez is neither an atheist nor a fundamentalist. His heart is in the right place. The film probes into conflicting ideologies between a father and son. Though *East is East* actually got Om noticed by the public and critics, it was in this film that Om felt he had excelled emotionally on screen.

Rachel Griffiths, the Australian actress played Om's love interest in the film. He had learnt that if your co-actor is better than you, then it is good for you. Rachel was hardworking, sincere and inspiring. She continually rehearsed with Om and generally made him feel at ease, besides suggesting new things. She even made it believable by behaving like his girlfriend off the sets!

Om is quite fond of Udayan and felt he directed the film sensitively. He is a gentle yet firm director who works with a lot of conviction. Although at times he can be stubbornly uncompromising. The film was dubbed in several languages worldwide and got Om a lot of visibility in the West. He was honoured as the Best Actor with the Crystal Star at the 25th Brussels Film Festival in 1998.

**Kurban**

Written and directed by Renzil D. Silva, Kurban was a unique experience because the producer, Karan Johar was very generous. The first thing he told Om when he visited the sets was, 'Om, please make unreasonable demands

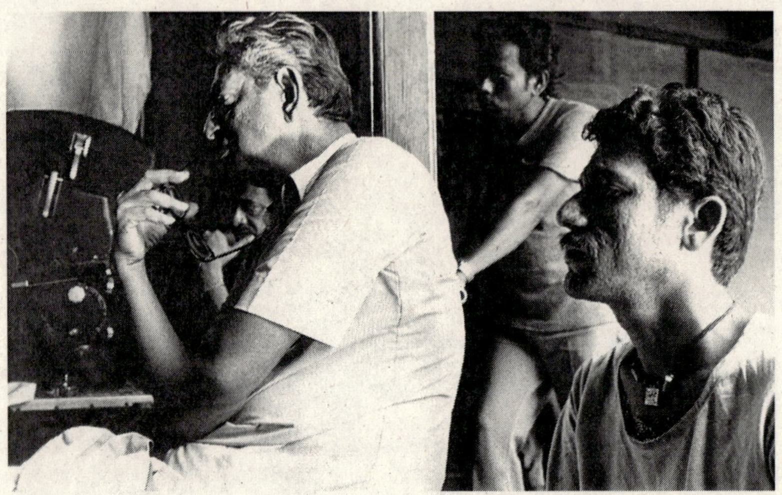

Satyajit Ray and Om Puri on the sets of *Sadgati*.

from the production.' This apart Om feels it was one of the most gripping screenplay….he read it like a James Hadley Chase thriller…he liked the surprises in the script. It was enjoyable working with Renzil as he is very focused and yet gentle though he can extract every last drop from an actor. And having seen *Kurban*, Om feels this film compares with the best of international cinema.

**Sadgati**

*Sadgati* was the first colour film made for Indian television. Satyajit Ray had seen *Aakrosh* and was keen to cast Om in this film. When Om heard his voice over the phone, he was literally trembling. 'I am sending you the script and I hope you like it,' the maestro's baritone boomed. Om thought he was being rather modest. Om met him the first time at the Raipur railway station. He was touched and honoured when the great man himself came to receive him. When he saw his 6' 4" frame towering over the rest, he remarked to his colleague, Mohan Agashe, 'Bade Mian himself has come.'

Manikda, as they called him, was every bit the Renaissance man. He involved himself in every aspect of filmmaking, from scripting to designing the sets and costumes to composing the music, storyboards to deciding the camera works – everything. He was very organized and meticulous about every last detail.

Om remembers on the first day of shoot he was extremely nervous. Manikda explained the scene to him. He was to walk into the Brahmin's house gingerly. Om felt awkward as he did not know the meaning of 'gingerly'.

With great effort, he asked him. He smiled and explained that 'when a dog or a goat enters an unknown house, he enters gingerly'. He not only explained it, he also gave him the body language to relate it with.

The hallmark of any great director is his openness to ideas which Manikda had. Once during *Sadgati*, Om suggested that Mohan Agashe who plays a Brahmin, would not touch his dead body directly as he belonged to a lower caste and was it okay if he used a rope to pull his corpse. Manikda thought over it and immediately agreed. This was the great Ray, who was known for not changing a line in his script.

**Sparsh**

*Sparsh* was perhaps the earliest and most sensitive of feature films delving into the lives and psyche of the blind. It was directed by Sai Paranjpe, an extremely liberated woman in the true sense of the term. She is one of India's first woman directors to make her mark in Indian cinema and working with her was an honour. Om's role was that of a blind teacher. As an actor, he was eager about playing a blind person and went about preparing for the challenging role. Since they were shooting in a blind school in Delhi, he began to follow the blind teachers and students a few days before the shooting.

One day a blind *sardar* student was asking his blind friend, '*Tune* Amitabh Bachchan *ki Sholay dekhi*? (Did you see Amitabh Bachchan's *Sholay*?)'

The irony in their words touched him.

The boys also enjoyed playing cricket. It was an enlightening experience. The cricket bats were a little broader than normal bats. The ball had a wire with some circular steel discs attached to it, so that every time a bowler bowled, the batsman could follow the sound of the ball and hit accordingly.

Those days in the blind school before and during the shoot made Om realize how innovative these boys could be. It made him question so many of his inherent prejudices about blind and disabled people and he emerged much the wiser from the making of that film.

**Susman**

*Susman* was shot in Mukhtapur, a small village near Pochampalli, the land of the famed *ikkat* weavers. In order to authenticate the role of a weaver, Om stayed in the village while the rest of the unit stayed in a hotel. Om would travel on a bicycle to a weaver's hut and had to learn to handle a loom. By the end of the film, he became half a weaver himself and wove forty metres of striped cloth, of which he made shirts and presented to friends, including Naseer, Alkazi *saab*, Safdar Hashmi, Govind and others. He wove four *dupattas* too, of which he gave one each to Shabana Azmi and Shama Zaidi and one each to his then girlfriends, Mala and Seema. When Om wove the first ten metres and presented to Shyam *babu*, he was very touched.

**Tamas**

Based on Bhisham Sahni's novel on the Partition, *Tamas* is one of Om's memorable films with Govind Nihalani. Govind wanted this to be his first film but it was not to be. It is four and a half hours long and was aired on television in four episodes. Unfortunately, due to its length, *Tamas* never got a theatre release but it was screened at the Montreal Film Festival with two intervals.

Govind is Om's Alkazi in Bollywood. Just like Ebrahim Alkazi was his mentor in theatre, Govind is his mentor in films. He is an actor's director. Om has given his life's best performances with him. Govind gets so involved in his work that at times during filming he forgets to call for lunch break if he is not hungry.

But he is a very greedy director and squeezes every last drop from an actor. Just like those sugarcane juice machines. Om jokingly told him that he is always hungry and '*bahut* footage *khata hai* (eats a lot of footage)'. He literally consumes raw stock like a maniac. After editing a Govind Nihalani film, one can actually make another film with the discarded raw stock!

Although Om does not always agree with him, he and Govind share a brotherly relationship. They both went to Czechoslovakia for the Karlovy Vary festival, which was the first trip abroad for both of them. It was a strange experience as there was sunlight till way past ten in the night and the food was very bland.

**The Ghost and the Darkness**

Om had seen and admired Michael Douglas' films, and was floored to learn that he was keen on having him in a film he was producing. *The Ghost and the Darkness* is based on a true story, *The Man Eaters of Tsavo* by John Henry Patterson, and was one of the largest Hollywood productions he has ever worked with. The film is based on a real story of two man-eating lions that caused havoc during the building of the railroad. Their stuffed heads can still be viewed at the Chicago Museum.

Douglas did not compromise on anything as he wanted the film to be perfect. He actually got two hundred Masai warriors flown down on location in South Africa for a single shot! And even Om's small role of the chief of the Indian workers' union could have been easily dispensed with but he preferred authenticity.

With Michael Douglas in *The Ghost and the Darkness.*

Om remembers the first time he met him was at one of the warm-up unit parties. He was sporting a ponytail those days. He strolled up to him and shook his hand and said, 'Hi. I am Michael Douglas.' Being an international star, that introduction was charming.

In one of the scenes, Douglas had to put a gun to Om's ear. Something went wrong and his ear got hurt. Douglas was extremely concerned. Later, when things were okay, he came up to me and joked, 'I nearly killed your husband.'

**The Parole Officer**

*The Parole Officer* was perhaps the only mainstream English film Om has done. Directed by John Duigan it starred Steve Coogan, the star of British television. Steve was extremely easygoing and fun to work with.

Om suffers from vertigo and one scene in this film terrified him out of his wits. He had to ride the world's second-highest roller coaster in Blackpool. Apart from riding the roller coaster he had to deliver lines with a jovial look as he was playing a keeper at the amusement park who has taken all the joyrides many times! He was so nervous he thought he would die of a heart attack and his obituary would read, 'Om Puri died on a roller coaster'. But finally he managed to pull through and survived the ordeal. As he came down, shaken, John asked him, 'Om, are you okay?'

He nodded, 'Yes.'

'Well, in that case,' John said, 'let's do a retake.' This time he nearly died of shock.

The funniest part about this scene was that he was supposed to enjoy the ride while Steve Coogan was supposed to look nervous in the shot and keep puking. In actuality, he loves roller coasters. Such is the life of actors.

**West is West**

The long awaited sequel to *East is East*, *West is West* begins where the former ends. Om's character, George Khan who was very aggressive in *East is East* is a much mellowed man here, knowing that his children have flown the coop and his didactic days are over. Here George Khan returns to his first wife and grown up daughters after thirty-five years. Whereas in *East is East* he escapes reality, in *West is West* he confronts reality and introspects on his past mistakes.

Mrs Khan No.1 is played by Ila Arun and instead of Pakistan, the film was shot on a location in Chandigarh. The film is funny with Ella, Om's British wife landing up unexpectedly. But it ends poignantly with the much anticipated meeting of Mrs Khan No. 1 and 2.

It took more than twelve years for Ayub Khan-Din to pen the sequel. Apart from the producer, Leslee Udwin and the make-up artist, Penny (to maintain continuity), most of the crew changed in *West is West*, including the director, Andy. Though Damien O' Donell was brilliant in *East is East*, Om did not miss him in this film as Andy was equally good. This apart Andy is extremely patient and gentle with his actors. One day when an actor could not remember his lines, Andy wrote out his lines on a big placard so that he could read and enact. An amusing thought occurred to Om then. Had it been Roland Joffe he would have killed the actor!

**Wolf**

Mike Nichols asked Om to play a cameo in *Wolf*, starring Jack Nicholson, Michelle Pfieffer and Christopher Plummer. This was an opportunity of a lifetime that Om could not resist. He had been a huge fan of Nicholson and this was a dream come true for him. Though Om appear in only one scene, it is a crucial scene where he shares screen space with Nicholson and he does most of the talking!

Jack works hard on each role and does not take his stardom for granted. He always had his lines ready before each shot. He and Om shared a common passion for smoking. So every time Jack would go out for a puff between takes, he would gesture to Om to join him in the 'bad boy's corner'.

Om played an eighty-year-old mystic in the film for which his makeup was done by three-time Oscar winning artist, Rick Baker. It was a pleasure seeing Rick work combining scientific precision with an artistic manner. He transformed his face and even he failed to recognize Om. The makeup took six hours to put on and an hour to take off!

The film was shot in Sony Pictures studio in Los Angeles. After *City of Joy* it was Om's second Hollywood film but the first in which he worked in a typical Hollywood studio. For the first time Om saw how everything ran with clockwork precision.

**Yatra**

*Yatra* was a great experience as Om got to see the whole country by train. Since it was a television serial sponsored by the Indian Railways, a whole train was given to Shyam Benegal and his unit to film for fifty days from Kashmir in up north to Kanyakumari in the extreme south of India. The concept behind this project was to show the diversity of the country and its different cultures through the unity of the railways.

Om's role in *Yatra* was of a kind of a narrator's or *sutradhar*, who held the unity of the different plots and characters together. By then Om was considered a mini-star and he got the only air-conditioned coupe among the crew. Shyam, who had a salon to be shared at times with his family, would on warm nights come and sleep in his coupe.

Om used to keep groceries in his coupe, had got himself a stove, and on days he did not shoot, even cooked. In the evenings, friends would gather in his coupe for a drink. Those days he used to drink Old Monk rum. Om also had a money plant growing in a bottle in the coupe to give it a homely feeling.

The concept was unique as the camera followed the goings-on with the characters travelling in the train exhibiting their cultural diversities. Whenever a place of interest came along, like the Sanchi Stupa or the Vivekananda Rock, the camera would leave behind the characters and follow that instead. If a particular shot was not okay, the train had to reverse a few kilometres to get it again. After fifty days there was a wrap-up party where every member of the unit joined in.

# That's *Amoré*

In any celebrity's life it is the women who come under deep scrutiny. And in his life story, the chapter that throws light on his relationship(s) with them is most eagerly awaited and read. Tabloids await the 'juicy gossip' while readers await 'revealing facts'. A biographer can and should make startling revelations about the men and women in his subject's life without making it sound vulgar or phoney. And this is exactly what I intend to do.

Om grew up in an environment almost devoid of women. His mother, Tara Devi was the only woman he knew for years until he reached his Mamaji's place in Sanaur. Moreover, Om's memory of his mother was of a 'grey and toothless' woman. In Sanaur too, there were no girls of his age and the only women he knew were his maternal aunts and the maids. So it was but natural for Om to take a liking to older women.

He must have been around fourteen when he was 'deflowered'. A fifty-five-year-old woman, Santi, used to provide general help in his maternal uncle's house. Twice a day, water was drawn into the house with a hand pump and Om was asked to assist Santi in the job. Days went by and Om kept pressing the pump backwards and forwards, till one day he realized that Santi would first touch, then caress and finally fondle him during the task. The young boy began to get turned on without knowing what was happening to him.

One day there was a power failure and in the dark, Santi grabbed Om, who was by then totally aroused. They slept together and the

Facing page: Ever the paramour of at least two women at a time, Om Puri strikes a mischievous pose.

fourteen-year-old felt really great having 'come of age'. Dark, greying, with a toothless grin, always dressed in half-torn *salwars*, Santi was Om's first lover.

❧

The fourteen-year-old's lust for Santi spilled over into a kind of attraction towards another older woman. This was his Badi Maami or older maternal aunt, Gomti Devi. Gomti Devi was childless and being a little more educated (maybe up to the fifth standard) than Satya Devi, the Chhoti Maami, she spent less time doing housework. So she was less frazzled and nice natured. Om remembers she was always attired in spotless white sarees and blouses and he warmed up to her the way most adolescents tend to do at that age.

It was perhaps this infatuation that led Om to caress the exposed navel of his other aunt, Satya Devi, one summer night on the family terrace under a moonlit sky. Though it was the younger aunt he was physically caressing, it was actually the aura of his older aunt that had overwhelmed him. The incident was probably the result of what is known as 'transference' in psychology – where emotions for one person are displaced or transferred onto another who is more accessible.

❧

Whatever the reason, his naïve act led to his shame and expulsion from the Kapoor household and Om was left to fend for himself. Soon after he started living with Kishan Singh, he developed a crush over a junior student called Savitri, whom he gave private tuitions. She lived close to the local *chakki* or grinding mill that was near his Mamaji's place.

Every now and then Om would carry ten kilos of wheat to the miller for grinding. He would look up from the corner of his eyes at her window to catch a glimpse of her. Just the sight of her with a *dupatta* draped around her shoulders was enough to make the young lad's heart spin. If she was not there, then Om would walk up and down by her house a few times like a fool, lugging the heavy sack of grain on his back.

Om was too shy to make a move and also feared her family's wrath. He was not sure whether she would reciprocate. But she definitely looked coyly at him as he went past her window several times a day. In fact, in order not to arouse the curiosity of neighbours, Om would begin to look up at her window from several metres ahead and after crossing her window did not turn to look back. But nothing materialized from it as Savitri was stoutly protected by her family.

Having to earn his own living from an early age and see himself through school and college, there was hardly any time left for Om to pursue romance. In NSD, though Om was more relaxed because he did not have to work, it proved a 'tough place' for a country bumpkin like him as he tried to learn to 'speak proper English minus the Punjabi accent'. But gradually he got into the groove with the NSD crowd and Jyoti, Jayshree, Rohini, Rita and Neelam were some of the girls he befriended.

Om's first crush was on Rohini, a talented and pretty theatre actress, who is now known for her role as Kasturba in Richard Attenborough's *Gandhi*. Despite knowing that she was dating a friend of his, Om overcame his shyness to go up to Rohini and profess his love for her. He vividly remembers her telling him that she was seriously in love with Jaydev Hattangadi (later to become a famous Marathi director) – and as she said this tears trickled down her dimpled face. She finally married Jaydev.

A loving picture of Om taken by Nandita just outside the kitchen in their home.

Sometime later Om developed a soft spot for Jyoti Deshpande, sister of the celebrated Marathi playwright, Govind P. Deshpande. But Jyoti turned Om down and was a bit haughty. His batchmate Jayshree, on the other hand, was kind and loving towards him. Soon Om reciprocated and started dating her. Gradually, Jyoti started to show some interest in Om. Now, Om could not let go of Jayshree's affections but he also did not want to turn down Jyoti. So he gladly began to date both though he admits he was extremely hesitant to commit to either. 'I was unsure about myself, about my future. To me relationships were serious and not just fly-by-night affairs. Besides, I was painfully shy and I guess my shyness did me in.'

Shy or not, Om was flattered by the attention he received from 'two educated city-bred girls' during his time at NSD, much as they relished his company. Jayshree remembers, 'Sometimes, he could be soft like a woman. And sometimes, he could look very handsome, like he did in *Suryamukh* and *Ibaragi*. He used to get so deeply involved in his role that he would even forget his lines.'

His classmate from NSD, Neelam Mansingh, remembers his talent for alluring women: 'A recurring image of Om in NSD was of being intelligent and quiet without being bold, and his friendship with two talented actresses … How he managed this threesome was a mystery to all of us and a source of endless gossip.'

When Om came to Bombay after FTII, he again got busy trying to make a living and women were out of consideration for a while, especially as they meant more expenditure from his meagre income. One day at the insistence of two friends who were visiting from Punjab (or so Om would like to assert), the trio set out to Grant Road, Bombay's famed red light district. The first time, Om admits he came back, having got cold feet. Second time round, he went in and instantly developed a liking for the young girl who serviced him. Her name was Rekha.

The next time he visited her, he took *paan* (betel leaf layered with spices and nuts) for her. The romantic in Om could not help himself. Rekha accepted the *paan* but a couple of times later when she realized

Facing page: The woman Om admired and learnt a lot from: Seema Sawhni, the enigmatic daughter of Ismat Chughtai and Shahid Latif.

that the young man was falling in love with her, she gently told him off by asking him to get married.

In any man's (or woman's) life there may be a series of romantic angles. They could be one-sided infatuations; platonic loves; one-night stands or fly-by-night affairs; and serious physical and emotional relationships. But the women a man dates or sleeps with are not always important to him. So, after having dated and known various women throughout his youth, it was ultimately four women who had a major influence on Om's life.

The first major 'love of his life' happened around 1982. While Om was staying as a PG in Ganga Vihar when Kulbhushan Kharbanda introduced him to Seema Sawhni, his girlfriend, who was a few years older to Om. She had seen *Aakrosh* and was impressed with Om's work. Seema was the daughter of acclaimed firebrand writer, Ismat Chughtai and filmmaker, Shahid Latif. A former airhostess, she was busy trying to make a career in advertising at the time. She was well-connected not only with the advertising crowd but also with the well-heeled South Bombay society.

It is said that opposites attract. Seema had all the qualities Om lacked and was to develop only later. Besides being attractive, she was intelligent, professional, extremely articulate and confident. While he was hesitant and shy and could barely express himself or his feelings properly. Om, of course, was immediately smitten by her charm and maturity. He found her very attractive as a woman and as a person.

Om remembers the first time Seema displayed her feelings when they were in Kulbhushan's Juhu apartment. Seema gave the inexperienced Om a full kiss on the mouth. 'For me it was the most divine kiss,' Om recollects. 'I was in paradise.' They started dating soon after.

For Seema, 'He just bristled! He bristled with curiosity, with ambition, with anger, with affection and love, but most of all, he bristled with talent.... I slowly realized that like an onion he had many layers and as they peeled off slowly, a person emerged who had managed to overcome an extremely difficult childhood and still had lots of love to give.... Even as success touched him, it touched him lightly.'

Seema was a divorcee and lived with her mother and teenage son close to Om's PG. She ran her house alone and her sense of independence impressed Om a lot. Om bonded well with her son, Ashish, though at times it seemed he resented his mother's proximity with Om. Om got along famously with Ismat *apa* and whenever Seema was away he would go to their house and enjoy the kebabs served by Habib the cook.

Within a couple of years, Om fell so madly in love, he wanted to marry Seema at all costs. (Something he became very cautious about in his future relationships.) But Seema wasn't considering marriage seriously after her turbulent experience. She savoured her independence and besides, she felt Om was more infatuated than truly in love with her. So she began to avoid him in a subtle manner. Om realized what she was doing but decided to give it a last shot.

Once Om was filming somewhere in South India and overheard someone mention that Seema was supposed to arrive there in a couple of days. Om had finished his shoot and had to pack up for Bombay.

On an everlasting love boat with Nandita on the Ganges in 1991.

'But I *had* to meet Her Majesty. She was the Queen Bee then. So I stayed on and paid the hotel fare through my pocket.' But when Seema arrived, she gave him a royal ignore and Om saw it was pointless to pursue her further.

Seema Sawhni was not only an important woman for Om Puri, but also a positive influence at a very vulnerable phase in his life. Her fierce individualism and tough spirit had taught Om enduring lessons for his future life in Bombay.

Around that time Om moved out of Ganga Vihar, but he often missed the hip and happening Marine Drive and his friends Subhash and Chinna. So, anytime he was in between appointments in town, he would drop in for a cuppa or even stay on for dinner. On one such occasion, cupid struck.

It was evening and after having tea, Om was leaving for Andheri when Chinna asked him, 'If you are going to Andheri, can you please drop Mala (Subhash's sister) at Dadar?'

'Sure, why not. It'll be on my way,' Om said gallantly.

Om was single, footloose and fancy-free. As they sat in the cab, on an impulse Om felt attracted to the pleasant-looking girl in a simple cotton saree who was talking enthusiastically about music. Gently, he placed his hand over hers. She did not shake it off. This emboldened Om and he told the cabbie to stop at Shivaji Park instead of Dadar, where they both got off. She seemed game for their little rendezvous but somehow 'both of us were feeling awkward to go behind the bushes'. So they walked hand in hand to her PG accommodation instead. On the way, Om bought himself a quarter bottle of Old Monk rum, which has been his standard drink for years.

None of her roommates was around when they reached, so Om had his usual peg at her place. The alcohol gave him further courage and he embraced her. And thus their long relationship took off. A relationship that Om has always cherished.

Mala had been in Bombay for a year or so when Om first met her and in spite of her sister-in-law's spacious apartment, Mala gave music tuitions and stayed on her own. A Bengali by birth, Mala had grown up in Benaras and spoke fluent Hindi. In fact, Om hardly ever heard her speak her mother tongue.

With Mala, who was a couple of years younger to him, it seemed that at last Om had shed his Oedipus complex. In her, Om found a simple and uncomplicated companion, who was educated, independent as well as homely. Mala was extremely caring and adaptable and also put up with his occasional philandering. She did not enjoy partying much and preferred to spend time at home. This suited Om because he was like that himself.

'In fact, one memorable New Year's Eve, we could not settle on where to go as every place seemed to be beyond our budget. Mala insisted we stay at home. Finally, we decided to give each other a pedicure. We got a bucket of warm water with soap and soaked our feet in together. It was one of the most romantic New Year's Eves I had ever spent.'

But there were times when Mala could be an embarrassment. She was not the sophisticated sort and at times would say the wrong things. Om was also socially shy but he was intelligent enough to hold his tongue. On such occasions, Om felt the need for a more socially savvy companion.

It was in the Trishul apartment that Om and Mala grew very close. They took a room for themselves and Bauji stayed in a separate room. Mala was able to get along with Bauji despite him being difficult at times. Bauji took no particular objection to her except that she left her hair loose. At times he gibed her by referring to her as the 'Bangalan' with '*khule huye baal*' (the Bengali woman with untied hair).

After paying off the loan for the house, Om was too broke to do up the interiors or furnishings lavishly. There was not even enough money to buy curtains. It was then that Om saw Mala's aesthetic talents come alive. She ingeniously converted some of her old sarees into curtains and put floor cushions instead of heavy sofas with bright mirror-work covers. Gurjari fabrics were both inexpensive and lent brightness to the ambience.

Since friends usually hung around on the terrace, Mala spread a couple of rugs, where they would spend evenings having rum and a simple *keema-pao* dinner, watching the polluted Bombay sky through the high-rises. Sometime later, when the basic furniture arrived, Mala got *chatais* from the Assam handloom store and stuck them on the bedroom closets. This gave them a unique touch and a classy look.

These little details impressed Om and he realized that with her artistic sense she could do much more than give music tuitions. Govind Nihalani was about to film *Aghaat* and Om requested him to let Mala do the costume design. Govind agreed and Mala put in a lot of hard work and enthusiasm. She managed a 'good job' according to Govind despite it being her first time. Govind then entrusted her with more of his important projects and later, Mala went on to win the National Award for costume design in Kalpana Lajmi's *Rudaali*.

Soon after *Aghaat*, all did not seem to go well with Mala and Om. Around that time, Om started bringing over his nephews to the city frequently and Mala felt she was losing her privacy with the boys hanging around the house throughout the day. Om felt his responsibility to his family came first. Then there was Bauji who constantly badgered Om to get married, which irritated Om no end.

But the biggest problem was Om's ambivalent attitude. 'I had a typical actor's problem. I wanted a steady girlfriend who loved me. And at the same time, I wanted to fool around with other women. Besides, at thirty-five, I felt too young to be tied down.' Mala, of course, did not share the same feelings regarding marriage. In her early thirties, which for Indian women was considered way over the hill, she wanted a husband and children. Every time she tried reasoning it out with Om, he begged for more leeway. Mala just got tired of his indecisiveness for more than four years where he kept her hanging inspite of her complete loyalty to him. Also fate intervened.

In the interim, Om had short-lived affairs with many women, mainly actresses from the theatre world, he continued to see Ranjit Kapoor's sister Seema off and on, especially when he visited Delhi. Despite Om's relationship with Mala, Om continued to see Seema, though he knew it was emotionally or morally not the done thing. Om admits he was under immense stress as far as both the women were concerned. There were qualities in each one that attracted him and he did not want to leave either. 'I wanted to marry both. I wish I could have done that. However, they would have none of my nonsense,' says Om.

Om, a traveller at heart, posing for a portrait in Paris in 1992.

Finally, Mala decided she had had enough of Om's wavering mind. Around 1986, she started dating one of his closest friends, actor Ashok Banthia. Ashok must have seen her through her worse days with Om. When Om found out he was devastated. All these years he had taken Mala for granted and assumed she would be with him despite all odds. When she actually walked out on him, he could not take it. He made up his mind to marry Mala.

Om, who rarely cries or pleads, just went to Ashok's house and begged Mala for forgiveness, fully aware how pathetic he appeared before them. But Mala would not relent. Worse was that it was around this time that Om was essaying the lead in Govind Nihalani's *Tamas*, where Mala was doing the costumes. It was a difficult time for Om as he had to see her and face his failure daily.

'I was so tortured with the thought of Mala having left me that in a month's time I greyed,' Om says, touching his more salty, less peppery head. And with his heart still longing for Mala, he was not able to commit to Seema, so he broke off with her. But it was the first time that Bauji showed his softer side to Om when he saw his son going through hell. Om had refused to come out of his room for days, so one day Bauji came and sat by him and ruffled his hair gently.

Though thoughts of Mala continued to haunt him for some time to come, he was happy when he learnt that she and Ashok had married each other. Om justified her happiness with the despair he had caused her. One thought related to her, however, embarrasses Om even today.

One day he read in the papers that the sets of Sanjay Khan's teleserial, *Tipu Sultan*, had caught fire in Bangalore. Among the actors caught in it were Khan himself, Neena Gupta and Ashok Banthia. A thought flashed through Om's mind: if Ashok Banthia were to die in the fire, Om would redeem himself and marry Mala and make up for all her heartache. 'Though it was only a thought, it stemmed from my strong yearning for Mala. Later, of course, I felt guilty for even thinking such a thing and was glad to know that Ashok had survived the fire. But at times, when the memory crosses my mind, I feel ashamed for wishing him harm.'

After Mala left him, Om got busy with work and his free time was spent looking after his nephews and Bauji. The house staff now consisted of a mother and daughter duo from Andhra Pradesh, Amma and her daughter Lakshmi. When they first came to Trishul, they stank a lot as they used to work in the local Versova fish market. It took a lot of coaxing on Om's part and several rounds of scrubbing with soap on their part to get rid of the stink.

Initially, Lakshmi and Amma used to serve part-time but seeing Om's hapless predicament with his nephews after Mala's departure, they stayed on to work full-time. Between them, they did all the housework and Lakshmi took pains to manage things well. Also, whenever Om was at home, she made extra effort to cook special food for him and walked around the house coyly. She even flirted with him playfully. Om did not fail to notice all this.

Lakshmi had a dark and voluptuous matronly appearance and Om found her suitably attractive. Thus their short-term physical relationship began. A few months later, Om realized that Lakshmi was getting quite attached to him. And since he was feeling grateful to her, on the spur of the moment, he decided to marry her. Not so much out of love, but out of a sense of idealism. He was inspired by his friend from his drama school days, Sreelatha Swaminathan. Sreelatha was an educated city-bred girl who, while working with an NGO, had married a tribal. Om thought he too could set an example for society. Or maybe he felt his reel life, where he acted out socially meaningful roles, should spill over into his real life.

'Thank God I woke up quickly from my idealistic stupor and did not commit to Lakshmi. We had nothing, absolutely nothing in common. If I was doing it out of a sense of revenge or guilt for Mala, then I would have been the sole sufferer,' Om says.

Lakshmi soon began to get very possessive about him. She would not pass on any messages to him from his female friends and would constantly question his whereabouts. Om did not like this and decided to terminate their short affair. Lakshmi, however, was not one to take it lying down. She threw a fit. And later, in front of him, she tried to climb onto the terrace rail and announced she was going to jump seven storeys down.

When Om pulled her back, she yelled hysterically, '*Nahin, mujhe marne do!* (No, let me die!)' Om could not have asked for a more melodramatic scene of a break-up than this!

Om had been friends with Seema for a long time, ever since her brother Ranjit Kapoor had come ten years back to direct a Majma play, *Bichchoo*. Seema was a young girl then, pursuing her graduation at Aligarh Muslim University.

Om found Seema to be a quiet and intelligent girl. Apart from singing, she was a voracious reader, wrote well, and had a way with words. All this drew Om towards her and on her first visit to the city he showered her with attention.

Much later Om caught up with her though they were in touch off and on.They were both nursing broken hearts and the inevitable happened: love on the rebound. With most of his friends having settled down, Om by that time was no longer feeling comfortable about nearing forty. He had already made up his mind about marrying Mala, and since that did not happen, his anxiety was growing. Besides, Bauji was getting on in age.

Om was finally keen to experience married life but he still harboured apprehensions about marriage. Seema convinced him to give it a shot. 'If it does not work out, we can separate,' she reasoned. Thus Om, the eternal ladies' man, decided to take the plunge.

They were married in February 1990 in her native town, Jhalawar. Om had very Hindi-filmish ideas about marriage. His idea of a *suhaag raat* or the first nuptial night crashed when he had to spend the night with Seema and a roomful of her relatives.

Om did not want any of the problems he had faced with Mala regarding his nephews, so he settled them at a nearby flat with Lakshmi looking after them, before getting married. Meanwhile, Amma managed the Trishul house.

Soon after his marriage, Om was invited to Rashtrapati Bhawan to receive his Padma Shri from the president. Om wanted to fly Bauji with him as he wanted Bauji to be part of that proud moment. At the same time, he wanted some privacy with his wife as it was going to be their first journey together after marriage. Taking this and the cost factor into account, Om let Bauji stay behind.

One day, a few months later, when he had just returned home, Om received a call from the Dadar police station informing him, '*Tere pitaji ko* taxi *ne udaiya.* (Your father has been knocked off by a taxi.)' Om was stunned. He rushed to KEM Hospital where they had brought Bauji. Thankfully, he was alive.

Om pulled all the stops to provide him with the best medical facilities. He first took him to the military hospital in Colaba and later shifted him to Jaslok. Bauji had broken his leg in the accident and due to complications of being hypertensive and diabetic, it had become worse.

In a lightsome mood in Mauritius with Shabana Azmi (left) and Soni Razdan (right) around 1985-86.

But as they say, the show must go on, so Om headed for Canada to shoot for Deepa Mehta's maiden film, *Sam & Me,* for which, Deepa had 'waited nervously for two days before he said yes'. Meanwhile, Ved and his wife came from Ludhiana to look after Bauji.

While Om was away, Bauji slipped into coma and was put on the ventilator. He never came out of it. It seems he was just waiting for his favourite son to return. Bauji passed away the day after Om returned from the shoot.

It had been Om's deep desire to take Bauji on a plane ride. To this day he regrets having missed the opportunity to do so. After the accident, Om had sworn to himself that when Bauji came out of hospital, he would take him to some holiday destination on a plane. It was not to be.

~

Barely had they celebrated their first anniversary that Om was disillusioned with marriage. In the twelve months of their life as a couple, Seema had hardly spent a few months with him. When he was away filming, she stayed on in Bombay. When he was in Bombay, she spent time in Jhalawar. Besides, Om found spending time with her family quite unnerving.

Again, Om's traditional film-inspired notion of marriage took a beating. He had felt it was a wife's duty to spend time with her husband. And while Om was still trying to get used to being a husband, it was a late marriage for her as well. They both needed space and time to adjust. 'But I had no patience then. I wanted it to be picture-perfect,' says Om.

Around a year later, Om landed one of the two lead roles in Roland Joffe's upcoming film. It was a big honour and the opportunity of a lifetime. He was required to shoot continuously for three months in Calcutta. As the unit was to be put up in the luxurious Grand Hotel in the city, Om thought at least now Seema would be happy and proud to be with him. 'I expected her to spend those three months with me. Instead, she left after three days. It infuriated me. This was not the marriage I had foreseen.

'At that point of time I guess Seema had lot of complexes. She abhorred social gatherings and spent time away from me. I felt rejected. She seemed a bit callous and bohemian in her attitude. Also, I felt I had probably rushed into marriage without really having gotten over Mala.

'Maybe I should have given her more time. But I was in a hurry yet again. This time because in Calcutta, I met a bright young journalist who came to interview me. Nandita was exuberant and lively and seemed the right blend of tradition and modernity. Though younger to me by sixteen years, she was the much-needed balm that was lacking in my marriage.'

This was indeed the most trying time in Om's life. His morality was put to the test. It was the third time in his romantic life that he was facing a dilemma, only, much worse. He had to either divorce one and marry the other or remain with one and let go of the other.

'I was concerned about both the women. While Seema's folks tried to reason with her to make amends, Nandita's pining for me nearly killed me with guilt. Finally, I took the tough decision. Maybe I was worried about Nandita being too young and vulnerable that I decided to tip the scale in her favour. Maybe I assumed Seema would be able to manage without me. She was, of course, very upset. And hurt. She refused to talk to me for years. Much later she told me, "I know I may not have been the ideal wife. But I don't think I committed that big a crime for you to divorce me without giving me a chance." I admit my guilt on that account. As also my meanness to her by falsely accusing her of crimes she was not guilty of. It was gracious on her part to leave quietly, swallowing her humiliation without creating a stir. However, seeing Seema finally making her debut as a feature director for NFDC, I feel happy for her.

'But at that time, it was indeed a difficult decision for me. The divorce came through in January 1993 and a few months later, I tied the knot for the second time with Nandita. It has been sixteen years since.'

K

# City of Joy

The year was 1991. The month, sometime in the middle of February. The venue, Calcutta. Fresh out of college, I had just started out as a cub reporter with the *Telegraph* as a freelancer. One fine morning, I glanced at the newspaper and wondered what news did a rickshaw-*wala* make to merit a front-page photograph? Looking closer, I saw the image of Om Puri, who was preparing for his role: that of the rickshaw-puller Hasari Pal in *City of Joy.*

The city was abuzz since the past few weeks as Joffe's unit was busy trying to film in the face of controversies and impediments created by the local Left Front government to stall the shoot. What impressed youngsters like me was the presence of Patrick Swayze, fresh from his *Ghost* and *Dirty Dancing* glory. We all secretly yearned to catch the superstar at a local disco sometime during the period of the shoot and shake a leg with him.

I remembered Om Puri as the horrific, pock-marked face in Biplab Roy Chowdhury's *Shodh*, chanting, '*Ek, ek bhoot, sau rupaiya*.' Then images of *Aakrosh*, *Ardh Satya* and *Tamas* flashed through my mind. Soon I forgot about it. Little did I know that this man would soon play a stellar role in my life.

A few days later, I was given a brief by my editor, Jojo (Jaideep Sen), who was looking after the colour magazine section of the *Telegraph*, to do a story on Om Puri and Shabana Azmi.

'Why not Patrick Swayze and Roland Joffe instead?' I remember asking rather cheekily, as I did not want to pass up a lifetime's chance of brushing with Hollywood celebrities.

Facing page: It was the filming of *City of Joy* in Kolkata that was to turn around Om's personal life forever. Here, he gives a ride to real-life rickshaw-pullers in a practice session.

The first photograph Om took of Nandita, who was taking his interview, caught her by surprise as Om was the one posing for her newspaper's photographer!

'No. You stick to Om Puri and Shabana Azmi for now,' Jojo said with an unmoving countenance in spite of my grimace.

When I called Om Puri, he politely granted me an interview, slated within the next couple of days. 'Shooting stalled, you see. CPM creating problems as usual. So I am free.' As I rang the bell of Room 460 of the Oberoi Grand Hotel, my first impression of Om Puri was, 'Hell, he is quite fair!' Having seen innumerable films of his where he plays a man from the labour class, I expected him to have been pulled straight out of a coal mine.

Om, on the other hand, loves to narrate this version of our first meeting: 'The bell rang and I opened the door. There was no one. Strange! I looked around. Then suddenly I looked down and saw this tiny young girl and I had to bend really low to say "hello" and tell her to come in.' Of course he loves to believe that he is really tall at 5′10″ and I am a dwarf at 5′1″!

Om was in the process of writing a letter to one of his nephews. He excused himself and said he would take a few minutes to complete it. I felt he must be a very considerate 'family man'. He then answered my questions and was articulate and sensible. He was extremely polite and charming throughout and what struck me the most was his

Om betrays his charm to Nandita as she takes his picture the same day.

simplicity and earthiness minus the starry behaviour (or my notion of it).

The interview was nearly over when my tape ran out. I told him I would return to complete it. I came back the next day along with the photographer, Pradeep Ghosh. While Pradeep was merrily clicking him, Om took a candid shot of me with his camera. Post-interview he offered us a beer. I almost refused but Pradeep wanted one badly and so we stayed back for a glass each.

A few days later Om called me at my office (the operator was speechless when she heard his baritone at the other end) and told me to come by for a cup of tea and collect the photograph he had taken of me. 'It has come out well,' he said. Over a cup of tea he showed me the photo. Till date I believe it is my best snapshot. Tea over and I asked him for the photo, and he said, 'Well, this stays with me. I shall make a copy for you. That means you will have to have another cup of tea with me.' He promptly stuck the photo on a framed painting in the room. I was flattered.

After that, Om would call up often and insist on exploring the cultural scene of the city. We went for a couple of classical performances but of course I soon realized he was not really interested in the cultural

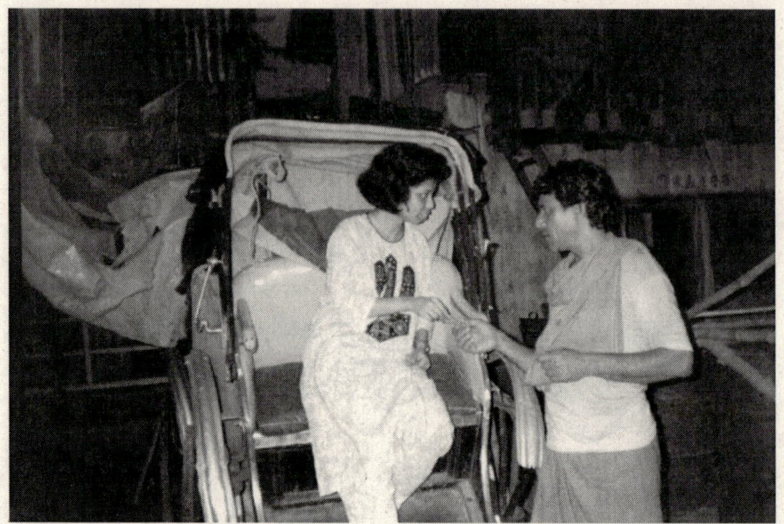

During their numerous meetings in Kolkata, Nandita visited the sets of *City of Joy*, where Om gave her a ride on his rickshaw!

scenario. I had also begun to enjoy his company by then. One thing led to the other and after several cups of tea and bowls of crispy rice soup in Room 460, I was madly in love with Om Puri.

The hitch in this love story was that Om was already married. He did talk of unhappiness and incompatibility in his marriage but then most men (and women) do. Initially, I was a little wary. Yet there was something about Om which made me trust him despite everything. It was a huge gamble. And I decided to play it.

With the end of the shoot it was time for Om to leave. I was nearly in tears. It was then that Om decided to take me to Nepal. 'It is the first holiday I am taking on my own. What the heck! After such a hectic shoot, I deserve it.'

Nepal was bliss. We did a tour of Kathmandu and Dhulikhel and trekked a lot. The latter, a tiny hamlet, was pure bliss with the clouds floating into our rooms. The setting was ideal for a full-fledged romance – the beautiful Himalayas as the backdrop in a strange country, where we both were freely afloat, not tied down by our daily lives or families. We put our best foot forward and Om bent over backwards to satisfy every little whim of mine. He even took me to a casino where I won a princely 600 rupees! It felt like a fairytale. And I, being as young as I was then, wished it would end like one too.

But from Kathmandu, Om flew to Bombay while I returned to Calcutta. The most painful period of my life began then. I felt he would forget about me as soon as he got busy with his work and responsibilities. I thought the honeymoon (sans marriage) was over and I was devastated. Worse, I could barely confide in my friends. They would not have empathized with me for getting involved with a married man. Moreover, I had to be careful about the media. I held on to the only thing I had – my belief and my trust in Om.

He did come back, and soon. Every month in between his shoots, he would come and spend a few days with me in Calcutta. We would sign in discreetly as Mr and Mrs Om Puri and I would shut myself in the hotel room for fear of meeting people I knew. It was also an extremely trying time for Om. He could neither live with me nor without me. Knowing Om now, he would have been the happiest to have all the women in his life live together in one big happy family with him as the sole object of their affection!

Two years hence, after several trips to Calcutta and many hours of long-distance phone calls between Bombay and Calcutta, Om and I settled down as man and wife on 1 May 1993.

~

May 1 is celebrated as May Day in Maharashtra. A holiday where all essential services are stopped. Obviously, then, the idea to celebrate our anniversary by taking friends out to dinner could never work out because liquor cannot be served in public places. So we began to stock up booze at home and settle for a relaxed evening year after year.

On the morning of our wedding day, Om realized that his car did not have enough fuel and we had to drive all the way to Worli to get married at a lawyer friend, Subhash Shah's house. So we kept the windows down and perspired all the way to Worli on the hot May Day.

We got married in the Arya Samaj way as Om wanted it to be a low-key affair. Om, who is not one for too many rituals, jokingly told the pandit, 'Cut the ceremony by half and I will double your fees.' Om's close friend, Neeraj Sharma and his wife, Chitra (also my friend), were there as well as Govind Nihalani. I wore a pink *tangail* saree and

Om wore a *veshti* (plain sarong for men). Most of my jewellery was borrowed from Chitra as I had left mine in Calcutta. The only pictures clicked were with an instamatic 110 camera by Govind Nihalani, also an ace cinematographer, who found it 'too complicated' after the 'simpler film cameras'.

Nearer home, on our return as a married couple, Om checked the petrol metre, glanced at an uncomfortably sweaty me, and pulled up the windows to turn on the air-conditioning. 'We are safe now. Enough fuel to reach home with the air-conditioning on.' That is Om, ever the pragmatic one.

Back home, Om called up a few friends and family to inform them about our marriage. Naseeruddin Shah, who had just landed from Delhi, turned up late at night with a bouquet of orchids. Another friend, Jayant Kripalani rang the bell way past midnight to wish us. He brought along with him the most ingenuous wedding present. A gift-wrapped broomstick!

My first morning as Mrs Om Puri started with me boiling the milk and spilling it over. Jayant's wife, Gulan interpreted that as a good omen to a new beginning.

A month after tying the knot, Om got an offer from Mike Nichols to do a cameo in his film, *Wolf.* Om by nature hates making guest appearances, especially in Hindi films, but if the director is Mike Nichols, your scene is with Jack Nicholson, and it is important to the storyline, then you would give anything to get a toehold into the project. Om had always been a fan of Nicholson. The producers gave him a first-class air ticket to LA which Om decided to split into two business-class fares, and we headed to Hollywood together. It was a simple honeymoon for me and a working honeymoon for Om. In future, we were to have many such working holidays.

I loved every bit of my US sojourn – from getting a peck on my cheek from Jack Nicholson to sitting with Nichols on the monitor and admiring Michelle Pfeiffer's beauty. We did the usual touristy things like visiting Universal Studios, the Farmer's Market, and the

Facing page: Om's co-actors, Shabana Azmi and Patrick Swayze on the sets of *City of Joy*.

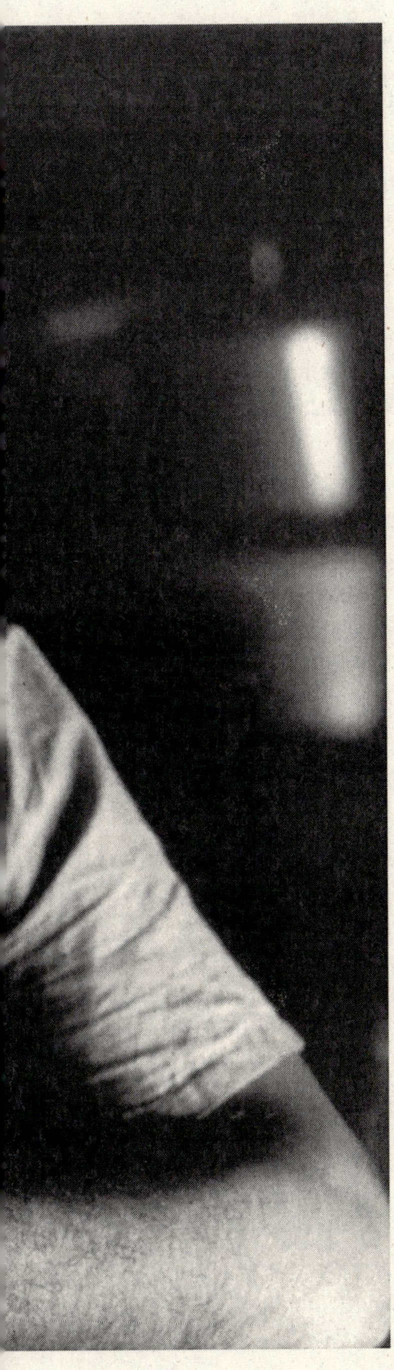

Huntington Library in Pasadena. I even managed to get lost in the Beverley Centre, as I had never been in a mall as big as that. Om almost died of fear when with shaking legs he checked every crossing to see whether I had been hit by a car. 'I had no idea how I would be answerable to your mother,' he thundered at me later. We almost got caught once for jaywalking as we had lost our way after a visit to Rodeo Drive. Because, as the guidebooks say, 'no one ever walks in LA'.

Back in Bombay Om got busy filming, literally working round the clock. He also brought his brother and *bhabhi* from Punjab and settled them all in a duplex penthouse in Bhayandar, on the outskirts of Bombay. Meanwhile, I got caught up trying to set up home. Like every other enthusiastic young bride, I was busy shopping furniture from Bombay's famous Chor Bazar or checking out upholstery at the various handloom stores. Full-time journalism had taken a backseat though I continued to write fortnightly columns that were mainly travel pieces.

Around 1995, Om got to be a part of another major Hollywood production: Michael Douglas' *The Ghost and the Darkness* directed by Stephen Hopkins. We flew to South Africa for the shoot. It was an interesting place to be in around that time as apartheid had recently been abolished.

Om's performance as Hasari Pal in the film got him noticed in the international circuit and won him immense critical acclaim.

Once we and a couple of white British girls from the costume department went to the nearby Nelspruit market and after shopping decided to drop in for a beer at a local pub. The pub was nearly full and buzzing. As soon as we entered, there was a sudden hush. Most heads turned towards us. It dawned on me that white South Africans were still not used to having coloured people invade their domain. But they could do nothing about it.

Once we decided to visit the nearby Swaziland for a Sunday lunch. At the border, as our passports were being checked, we saw that a number of our unit members were being freely let into the tiny kingdom. After an hour's wait we asked what was wrong. We were directed to a notice which clearly stated that Indians, Pakistanis and Bangladeshis were not welcome. Apparently, people from the subcontinent do not have a very good track record abroad. We managed to go to Swaziland sometime later and sample the great seafood there, not because we were particularly keen but because Om had suddenly became adamant. 'I want a Swaziland stamp on my passport,' he said with childish fervour.

~

This time, on our return to Bombay Om was enthusiastic about starting a family. But I was happy being footloose and did not want to get tied down with children immediately, so it was deferred. The house was a bit bare except for the three tortoises, Amar, Akbar and Anthony that Om had got from the sets of *City of Joy*. With enough time on my hands, I began to look after the stray dogs in and around my area.

One day, a little pup barely a couple of months old, infested with ticks and fleas started following me around as I used to feed him milk and bread every evening along with the other strays. He looked mangy and weak. On an impulse, I decided to bring him home. Om was having tea on the terrace. 'Who is this?' he asked.

'Can I keep him for a few days? He is too weak and might die if left alone. Once he is a bit strong, we'll let him go,' I pleaded.

'Okay. But what's his name?'

'Jackie,' I replied, taking the name the children in our neighbourhood had given him.

The first thing I did was to rub tick powder all over Jackie. Jackie did the dance of his life as he was in pain because all the ticks stung him before dying. Seeing Jackie's predicament, Om laughed his head off.

'Will you stop it,' I admonished.

'It is one of the most hilarious sights ever,' Om said, laughing.

A few days and then a week passed and not just me, Om too got very attached to Jackie. 'Do we really have to send him back,' he finally said. I was just waiting to hear that.

And so Jackie came to stay with us. We behaved like new parents, pandering to his every whim and talking incessantly about his pranks to friends, who actually got bored stiff, but out of sheer politeness suffered the overdose of 'Jackie stories'. Some even mistook Jackie the dog for Jackie Shroff, the actor, during conversations.

Once while filming with Jackie Shroff, Om asked casually, whether Shroff had a dog. He replied he didn't like dogs too much and did not intend to keep one.

'But you must,' Om insisted.

'Why?' Shroff asked.

'Because then you can call him "Om".'

Shroff looked bewildered and thought Om had gone crazy. 'But why would I do that?'

Om smiled mischievously and said, 'You see, I have a dog called Jackie.'

Shroff almost got up to hit him!

Jackie became an integral part of our lives and whenever Om returned from a shoot, even if he was ten minutes away from home, Jackie could smell him and squeal in excitement, running around the place. When our son was born, obviously our attention to Jackie diminished a bit. But he took it sportingly. As Ishaan grew up, he more than made up for it by petting him silly. He always called him Jackie *bhaiya*, giving him the respect of an elder brother. After twelve years of staying with us Jackie died in October 2007 of an enlarged heart. Om was away in Chandigarh and unfortunately could not get back in time to give him a teary 'send-off'. Even now he misses 'the little bugger' who would welcome him wagging his tail at any time of the day or night.

# Heads and Tails

1997 was a landmark year for Om. He became a father when Ishaan was born and survived against all odds. That in itself was a cause for celebration. It would have seemed that with the birth of Ishaan, Om's work pace would slow down, but he worked with even greater gusto. It was also the year of Om's debut as a hero in Bollywood's commercial venture, *China Gate*.

The director of *China Gate*, Rajkumar Santoshi says, 'It was during *Aghaat* that Omji first pushed me to chart out on my own as a director. He would tell Govind to my embarrassment, "Throw him out of your sets. He has to become a director." He even offered to act in my first film in whatever capacity and kept his word. Whenever I wrote a script, Om Puri was my Dharmendra and Amitabh Bachchan.... that is the kind of faith I have in him.'

The best thing that happened to Om in terms of a career boost was *East is East*. Later the next year when Om called up from Cannes, saying that 'the standing ovation after the screening seemed never-ending', we realized the enormity of its success. Many other films followed, including popular television films like *White Teeth* (based on Zadie Smith's novel), *Second Generation* and *Canterbury Tales*. These telefilms for the BBC and Channel Four were also responsible for making Om a household face in the UK, where he worked for the next eight years or so. Being away in England for the major part of the year, filmmakers in India assumed he had settled there. And people in England wondered why he had to go back to Bombay every time. 'Don't you live in London?' they would ask, surprised.

Facing page: Om, Nandita and their son, Ishaan walking the red carpet at the Monte Carlo festival in 2006.

The family takes a ride on a rickshaw in Malacca, Malaysia, in 2006.

The director of two of his British films, *Brothers in Trouble* and *My Son the Fanatic*, Udayan Prasad, said of him, 'He has a huge presence on the screen. The camera just loves him. If you are sitting with Om Puri you better be good, else nobody will be looking at the other guy. Om is the best known Indian actor in Britain of his time apart from Shilpa Shetty. Personally, I would liken him to Gene Hackman.'

Earlier on, Mike Nichols had also said about Om: 'He was brilliant (in *Wolf*) and made many things believable through the powerful presence and with his special kind of detail that is unmatched by any actor I know.'

Before Om, Kabir Bedi and Saeed Jaffrey had tried their luck in English films. But they couldn't really make their mark due to the colonial attitudes that were still prevalent at the time. After *City of Joy*, Om got himself accepted by one of UK's top screen agents, Jeremy Conway, who has been quietly advising Om regarding his projects in the West for more than a decade now.

More than anything else, Om was never under the illusion that after a lead role in an American film, he was the next big import from

With Nandita in front of Blenheim Palace, UK, Winston Churchill's birthplace.

India for Hollywood. 'The first thing I told Jeremy was I may call you once in a while. But mainly to say hello or wish you a happy New Year. I will not push you to find me work. My acting shop is running well in India, so whatever I do abroad will be a bonus.' It was this winning attitude which endeared him to Jeremy.

In Jeremy's words, 'I am happy to be part of Om's success story, having collaborated with him in shaping his career in the West. But the credit goes to him as he is an amazingly good actor. After seeing *City of Joy*, I felt he essayed the role so realistically. He hardly acted. He has an amazingly strong face which gives his roles so much character.'

And as Leslee Udwin, producer of *East is East* succinctly put it, 'I had heard of Om being described as the "Robert De Niro of India" and that is a magnificent compliment, really.... Om Puri commands international respect in the sense that you can cast Om Puri and the film will get funded.'

Those were fun times for the family, spending months together in various apartments in London like Notting Hill, Holland Park and

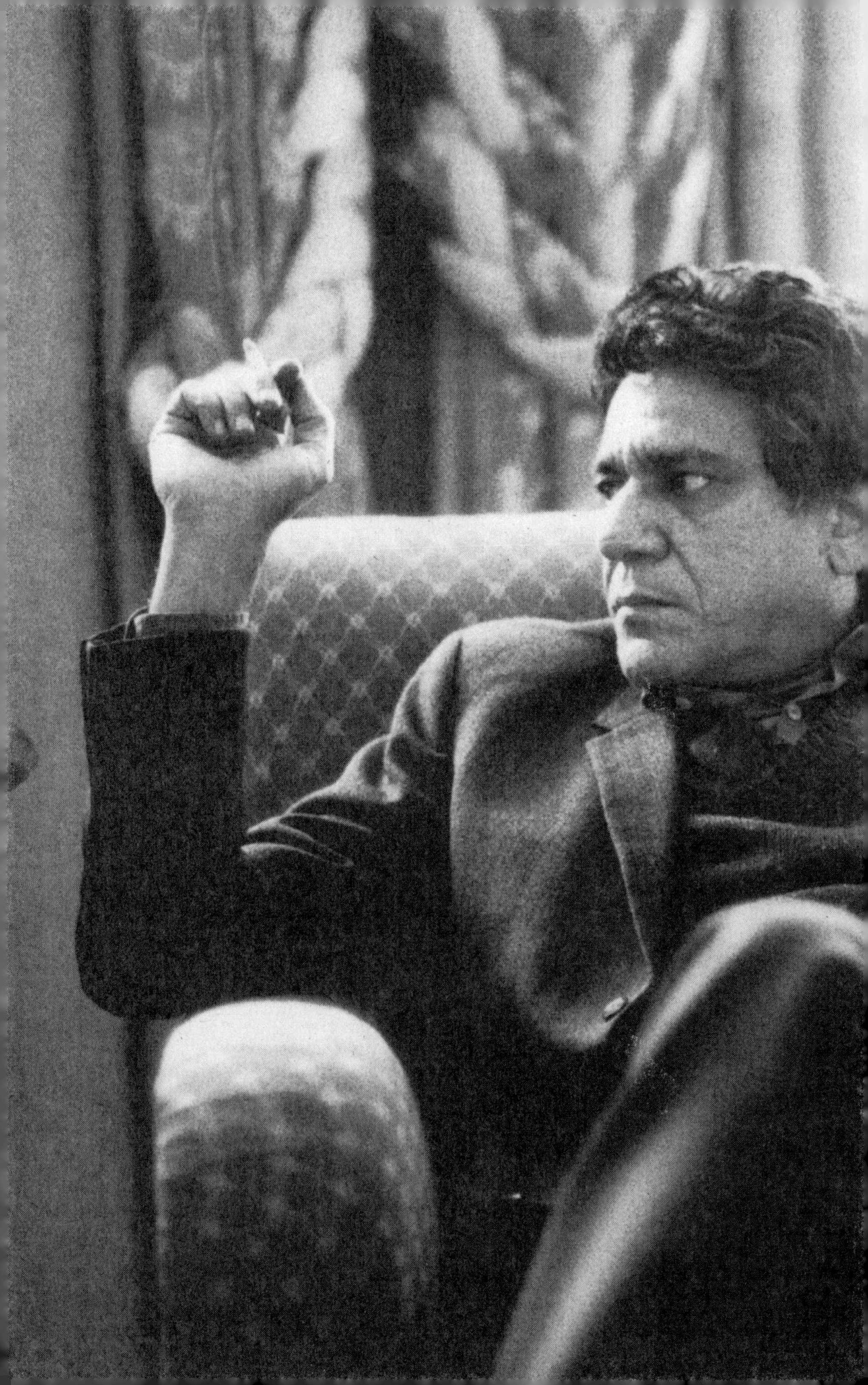

Om resting during a shot on the sets of *My Son the Fanatic.*

Om and Ishaan dressed up in traditional Egyptian *galabiya* dress for the fun Galabiya Night on the Nile Cruise.

later, Kensington. Ishaan enjoyed his frequent sojourns so much that once when we had not been to London for more than six months, he innocently told Om, 'Baba, this weekend let us skip Khandala. Let us go to London instead. We haven't been there in a while.'

Another memorable trip was to North Wales in the freezing month of December when we joined Om for the filming of *Happy Now*. Our friend Sadhana Rao and her son Arnav joined us. When Om had to go for a radio interview to Birmingham, Sadhana and I decided to take the children out to Cadbury's factory. Next day, when we came down to breakfast, we saw that Ishaan and Om had been awake since early morning and the proud father boasted how he had fed Ishaan a hearty meal. 'He has had a banana, an egg, milk and couscous, cooked by me.' And all within the space of two hours – it was remarkable as Ishaan is an extremely poor eater.

Barely a few miles out of winding Barmouth, Ishaan got his emperor's breakfast out. Om turned back to leave us at the apartment before Ishaan could drop any more of his meal along the way. All our hopes of seeing the chocolate factory were dashed. 'Om should not have stuffed him thus,' I exchanged these sentiments with Sadhana who seemed to agree knowing Ishaan's poor appetite. Om always feels

Ishaan should look like a '*hatta-katta* Punjab *da puttar*' (a strong and healthy Punjabi boy) like his grand-nephews and nieces. However, Ishaan continues to defy the Puri tradition.

Another time Om took us to Legoland and enjoyed every ride with childlike glee. When he was shooting for the film *The Zookeeper* in a Serbian zoo in Prague, Om took Ishaan around, showing him lions and gorillas, to the child's sheer delight. Another memorable trip was a coast-to-coast US tour organized to promote *East is East*. Apart from walking the red carpet (Independent Jury Awards) and rubbing shoulders with Hollywood stars, we also got to stay in some of the best hotels including the Trump Towers and the Ritz Carlton in San Francisco.

Once, early morning, Ishaan was up and looking down at the street from the seventeenth floor of Soho Hotel in New York. Suddenly, he announced, 'Look! Yellow car. Now blue car. See! Red car. Yellow car again!' I ran to the window and saw that he was bang on about the colours of the cars as they whizzed by. Om too shot up from the bed and asked whether Ishaan was announcing the colours correctly. I nodded. We both were ecstatic. A couple of years earlier, Ishaan had been diagnosed with severely damaged retinas. We were not even sure whether our son would be able to see at all. That morning was the best moment of our trip.

Soon after, Om started working with a cross-section of varied and dynamic Bollywood filmmakers and actors, like Vishal Bharadwaj in *Maqbool* and Priyadarshan in *Hera Pheri*, where he proved his flair for comedy. In fact, long before, the director of *Jaane Bhi Do Yaaro*, Kundan Shah had remarked: 'Some gifted actors are always larger than the roles they play on screen. Om Puri does not quite fit into this category but manages to do something equally great: he becomes the role.... Even in his comedies, none of the characters is a caricature. He has breathed life into each role and made them so memorable and unique that you sympathize with them. What more can a director want?'

And after working with him, Priyadarshan said, 'He is perhaps the only actor who does not lose his cool on the sets, even if he is feeling ill

Om Puri with friend and co-actor of *Chachi 420*, Kamal Hasan.

or ill-paid. Off-screen we share a healthy brotherly relationship. Sometimes he behaves like a child. He is the only Indian actor who is perhaps a bigger star abroad than here.'

For Bharadwaj, however, it was a completely different experience: 'He is one of the rarest actors and I have grown up watching him and Naseer.... I was thrilled to be directing them both in *Maqbool.* There was this scene where they, essaying two corrupt cops, decide to take a free ride from a cabbie. Omji called me aside and told me that when they return the cabbie's license, they must warn him not to park in a "No Parking" area. These little touches show his minute sense of observation.'

Some of the actors he worked with around this time included Amitabh Bachchan, Kamal Hasan and Paresh Rawal. With Kamal he shared more than a professional camaraderie and Hasan himself feels the same: 'More than colleagues, Omji and I share fraternal feelings.... To me Om and Naseer are not just actors, but true stars. Once while in London, I saw a poster of *East is East* and I promptly got myself photographed next to it.... I try to write him into a film whenever I can.'

At the Locarno film festival with Ismail Merchant and Anita Desai (front row); Shabana and Nandita (second row); and son, Ishaan.

On a personal note, Paresh Rawal had said: 'The kind of actor that Om Puri is, the world knows. But the kind of warm person he is, I found out during the shoot of *Malamaal Weekly*. It was a horrendous place and the unit food was the pits. He used to personally supervise in the kitchen, go to the market and feed us. A great actor does not always have to be a great person, but Om's concern for his fellow actors, opened up a new vision of him for me.'

2004 was to bring a major change in Om's life. Since a few years he had been suffering from severe backaches, which seemed to worsen as days went by. Earlier on, soon after *City of Joy*, he had suffered leg pains. It had then been attributed to the rigorous regimen of rickshaw-pulling. But the reasons for the backaches were many, the foremost being the backbreaking stunts Om did without using a double in several films. Sometimes, in annoyance, Om also likes to attribute it to the heavy luggage he had to lift at airport conveyor belts, 'full of your junk shopping'.

In December 2003, Om decided to take us to Punjab to revisit his childhood village. We stayed with the Tiwanas in Patiala. Om met up with his cousins and their families after a gap of thirty-odd years. We visited Sanaur, where Om showed Ishaan his old school and visited the house of his farmer friend Kishan Singh. Kishan had died but his family was there. With a lot of changes and new construction, Om had a difficult time locating old houses and lanes.

One morning, soon after breakfast, Om's knees buckled as he was walking in the garden. The doctor told Om to rest and go to Bombay as soon as possible for treatment. We left for Chandigarh, where we stayed at his NSD classmate, Neelam Mansingh's house and Om tried a few days of acupressure treatment. However, when things did not improve we headed to Bombay. Here, veteran neuro-physician Dr B.S. Singhal advised immediate surgery. Om called up Shahrukh Khan on reaching Bombay, who was recovering from a similar surgery, and left for London to be operated on by the same surgeon as Shahrukh's – Professor Alan Crockard at the National Hospital in London.

The repercussions post-surgery were quite bad. Om was assured that he would be able to resume normal activities in a couple of months. Instead, it took him almost a year and a half. Even then, he had lost the sensation of his lower limbs for some time and walked with a limp for the next two years.

'In fact, every step is an effort. I feel like I have weights strapped onto my knees. Earlier I could walk ten kilometres at a stretch easily, today I'll be happy if I can achieve a third of that. I never thought I would walk like a seventy-five-year-old at the age of fifty-five.' For someone who had hardly ever fallen ill and was a workaholic to the core, Om's self-confidence took a severe beating as well. The surgery coincided with his andropause and Om went into deep depression and mood swings. Again, on the advice of Dr Singhal he consulted Dr Asith Sheth, a well-known psychiatrist who with advice and medication managed to bail him out of that period.

According to Dr Sheth, 'Depression and physical illness were alien concepts to Om but being of strong disposition he recovered quickly. Behind his tough exterior he is sensitive. I have handled many Bollywood personalities but found Om to be quite humble.... Om recovered due to his never-say-die attitude and that is Om Puri for us.'

On the other hand, Om realized: 'We actors take our bodies for granted. Till illness hits us, we do not learn to value them. For years I have tried to give up smoking but I just lack the will. When my son makes an effort to stop me from smoking by hiding my cigarettes or throwing them away, I feel touched and sad, but helpless. When the doctors advise me to quit, I try but lack the determination. Then again I take the easy way out and I console myself with examples like Churchill's. He smoked like a chimney and drank like a fish and lived till his ripe old nineties!'

With Tom Hanks, Nandita and Ishaan during the shoot of *Charlie Wilson's War* in Morocco in 2006.

Om's physical and mental condition inevitably affected our family life. Ishaan understood that his father could not prance around with him like earlier times. Something was wrong with Baba's back and it made the little fellow a little insecure for to Ishaan his Baba was the 'strongest'. His bouts of bad mood came onto me the most. Although I tried to keep my cool, at times I too lost patience. But the worst sufferer was of course Om himself. His pain and frustration were beyond explanation and as much as friends and family tried to sympathize, the burden was his alone to bear.

Despite his pain, Om took a trip to Jim Corbett National Park with

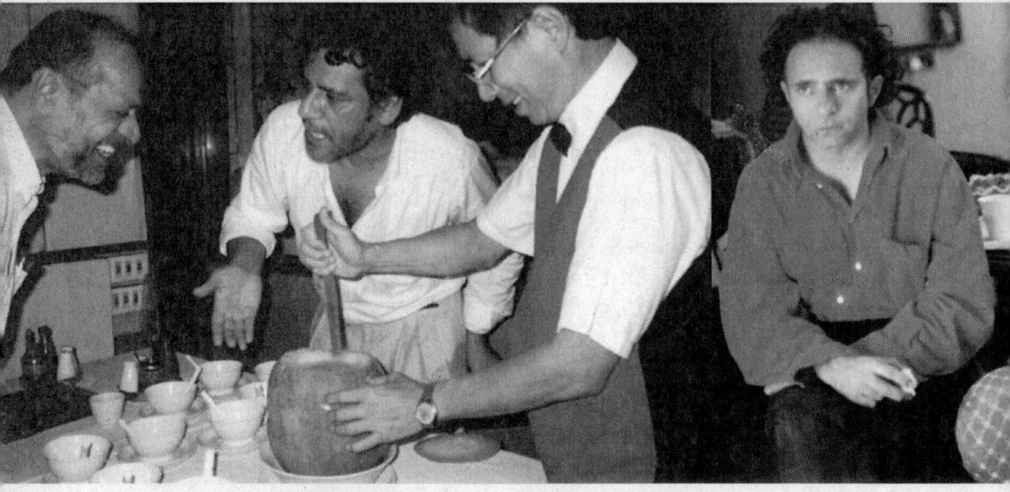

From L to R: Shyam Benegal cracks up as Om comments on the pumpkin soup they are about to eat; The maverick among British cinema scriptwriters, Hanif Kureishi, and Om on the sets of the critically acclaimed, *My Son the Fanatic.*

his environmentalist friend, Bittu Sahgal. Bittu recollects, 'Neck brace in place to guard damage to his spine, Om Puri bravely plunged into the world of wildlife when I invited him to visit Corbett with me.... The next morning in the forest Om was like a kid in a candy store. He was mesmerized but aghast that such beauty needed so much effort in protecting. He befriended guards, drivers, mahouts and other "ordinary people". There is an ability of connecting with people irrespective of who they are or what they do ... He can drink more than I can. Also his vocabulary of colourful expletives is infinitely more evolved than mine!'

Because of the support of doctors, staff, family and a few genuine friends, Om was able to come out of this period a lot saner. Dr Singhal said wisely, 'You cannot mourn forever over the damage to your knees. Don't further damage your sanity by doing that. Just dive headlong into work for I can sense you are a man who is happiest working.'

Several times Om called up Shahrukh, who had been through the same ordeal. Shahrukh told him, 'I know the feeling is rotten. But you have to forget it and involve yourself in life and living. Laugh and the world laughs with you. Cry and you cry alone, Omji.'

With Naseeruddin after being made an officer of the Order of the British Empire (the OBE can be seen on Om's *kurta*) for his contribution to English cinema.

After a gap of nearly two years Om resumed work like before. In the interim he refused a lot of films because of the post-surgery recovery. Among some of the coveted roles was that of Preity Zinta's father in *Veer Zara* and a character based on Adnan Khashoggi in George Clooney's *Syriana*.

But the milestone that came his way was well-timed and cheered him up. HRH Queen Elizabeth II made him an officer of the Order of the British Empire in her birthday honours in 2005. For the scrawny lad from Patiala, who had a complex about his poor English at drama school, Om Puri had indeed traversed a long road to success.

One balmy evening, while sitting over drinks on our terrace, his friend and colleague of nearly four decades, Naseeruddin Shah summed up the honour thus: 'I was always the missionary school educated upstart who spoke impeccable Queen's English. And here we had Om Prakash Puri, who barely managed to speak English and that too with a heavy Punjabi accent. It was a foregone conclusion that I would excel in all things English, be it theatre or cinema. And leave the vernacular field to my friend here.

'But today in 2005, look at the irony of it all. Om Puri, who could

With friends and colleagues from all over the world. On a break during the shoot of *The Parole Officer* with Omar Sharif (left); with Damien O'Donnell, director of *East is East* and Ismail Merchant in New York (right).

not speak English properly, gets an OBE from the Queen for his contribution to English cinema. And I, Naseeruddin Shah, have been honoured this year with the Padma Bhushan for my contribution to Indian cinema. I am not complaining though.'

His co-actor of many films, Shabana Azmi agrees: 'Om is a tree that is rooted firmly in the villages of Punjab whose branches have become wide enough to spread and embrace the Western world. Yet he has never counted his laurels. He has rather underplayed it.'

The year 2006 started with Farhan Akhtar's remake of *Don* in Malaysia. Ishaan and I accompanied Om throughout from Malaysia to Singapore to Canada and Scotland on various shoots. In July that year he was called in to be a member of the jury at the Monte Carlo film festival and later we visited Morocco for the film *Charlie Wilson's War* by Mike Nichols.

In 2007, Om and Naseer were honoured as Indians who had contributed much to the arts, at the Nehru Centre in London, after a tête-à-tête with a select Indian audience that included a reading from my debut book of short stories, *Nine on Nine*. Om also accompanied me to successful readings of the book in major Indian cities including the prestigious Calcutta Book Fair.

Above: Om on the sets of *Wolf* with Nandita, wearing the makeup for his role, which took six hours to put on and one hour to remove! The makeup was done by the celebrated Rick Baker, who used to be Michael Jackson's makeup man.

Right: With Jack Nicholson and Nandita in Los Angeles, during the shoot of *Wolf* (Mike Nichols) in 1993.

Om and family having a fun time in Egypt in 2008.

Currently, he is busy doing the usual Bollywood fare: some very interesting and some run-of-the-mill. In the midst of all this Om was appointed chairman of the almost defunct NFDC (National Film Development Corporation). He was initially sceptical, especially after the various financial scandals NFDC has been plagued with in the past few years. Moreover, his friend Manmohan Shetty who preceded him in this honorary post did not have a pleasant stint. But NFDC badly needed a name to up their image and Om having acted in several good NFDC films of yore (including *Jaane Bhi Do Yaaro*) decided to step in as chairman if it helped the latter.

Om rarely takes a holiday when shooting abroad. Last summer, however, he took the Nile Cruise from Aswan to Luxor for five days,

Father and son pose before the Obelisk in Aswan in Egypt.

before reaching Cairo for the film *Singh is Kinng*. In the cruise he participated in most of the activities including wearing a *galabiya* for the Galabiya Night. The best compliment he received was when a few locals asked him whether he was Egyptian. I think it was because of the mobility on Om's face. His features are, as Jeremy says, 'pan Afro-Asian and Middle Eastern'.

Egypt had been our dream destination and we all looked forward to it. It was after a long break since his surgery that Om had regained part of his enthusiasm for roaming like a normal tourist. This enthusiasm pleased Ishaan the most. Om accompanied us in the searing heat to the Valley of the Kings and Queens, Philae Temple, Karnak Temple and the Cairo Museum till he exasperatedly exclaimed, '*Mujhe ek aur patthar nahin dekhna hai!* (I do not want to see yet another stone!)'

Dog and master blissfully asleep at home. Om could not resist adopting Jackie, a stray pup, after it had spent a week recovering under Nandita's care in their house.

# Om at Home

This is perhaps the most difficult chapter of the entire book. Perhaps it is this chapter alone that has been the cause of this book incubating for nearly fifteen years. And yet, it is this chapter that will make this into a well-rounded biography as it will add layers and reveal the man behind the actor.

Being a journalist of conscience, I have been brutally honest in my columns even to the point of annoying my friends. But in writing this, I had to tell my husband's story and tell it engagingly without being provocative or partial. At the same time I could not mask the truth. It was a strange predicament.

Writing about one's parents, siblings or children is far easier than writing about one's spouse. In the case of a marriage, the couple starts off as friends and lovers and then forms a certain relationship where they get to see the best and the worst of each other. To the world a person may be a great human being, a helpful colleague or an eternally smiling friend. Back home he lets his guard down. He becomes his true self.

Tantrums emerging out of his anger and frustrations initially witnessed by his parents are subsequently borne by his partner because they have become so close. Such moments call for the wisdom to be silent, to ignore the impetuous remarks, and try to understand the pain behind them. Was it not Browning who wrote, 'Grow old along with me! The best is yet to be'? And that is how enduring marriages are made on earth.

Facing page: Om, the 'food-fixer', as Nandita calls him, cooking chapatis.

This biography, about an actor who believes in the honesty of his craft, had to naturally reflect the professional aspect. But being a biographer who was living with her subject and saw him at his weakest moments, I had to subdue my personal opinion and strive to write objectively as well. It was a fine line I had to tread.

Om has very set ideas about what should be written about him. So when fifteen years ago he told me he would sponsor me to write a biography on him, I held back on two counts. One, I was a fresh writer with stars in my eyes regarding the subject and felt deep down that I would not be able to do an honest job. It would only end up being one long eulogy! The one you read at funerals. And one people are mostly likely to pass over with a smirk.

The second reason was, I hate the term 'authorized' in biographies. It implies you have written them according to the subject's point of view, who then becomes the 'author', not you. Nothing is unidimensional. More so, life and relationships. And Om has not always been very conducive to opinions which were not very flattering to him. Om loves

Om at home! From left to right: Enjoying a tête-à-tête with Nandita; in a masti mood – Pradeep Upoor (on the left) and Pavan Malhotra watch the fun; with baby Ishaan in lap and Nandita.

to be honest but at times his honesty is selective. So, I chose to hold back till I knew him well and could tell his story better.

This time round when Om sat for this book with me, narrating his story and experiences over several long periods, he managed to overcome his diffidence and was sometimes even brutally honest. There were times even I had to ask him whether he was sure he really wanted to tell what he was saying. He nodded a yes with a 'I want to be as honest as possible' look. Other times, he asked me to change a few facts here and there, as he did not want to be harsh to some people, especially the women in his life.

There is an old Arab proverb that says, 'The words of the tongue should have three gatekeepers.' The first gatekeeper asks, 'Is it true?' That stops a lot of traffic immediately. Once you get past this gate, then the next gatekeeper asks, 'Is it kind?' And finally if you pass this one, the last question is, 'Is it necessary?' I try to abide by these qualifiers whenever I write.

When we first started dating, Om used to call me N*on*dita, emphasizing the Bengali accent. He even wrote it as Nondita in his love letters to me. Over the years, my name has taken on a more Punjabi accent – Nand*itta*!

Initially, I would get a little shocked with his Punjabi expletives. To get me used to it, he would suddenly call me with urgency; and when I rushed to him, he would have a wicked gleam on his face and say, '*Teri* ...'

One night, just as we retired, he got up saying, 'Oh shit!'

Concerned, I asked, 'What?'

And he replied, '*Teri* ...'

He has caught me unawares like this many a time but now I have wizened up to his pranks.

Yet, I must admit he has me foxed when he rehearses his lines.

'Have you got the money?' he would ask suddenly.

'What money?' I would respond, sheepishly realizing that it is his lines he is rehearsing and not me he is talking to.

The authenticity reflected in his acting can be slightly unnerving.

Having excelled in tragic roles on-screen, Om loves to play the protagonist off-screen too. In all his failed relationships, he always paints himself to be the wronged rather than the wrong one. And people tend to believe him. That's the flipside of being married to a very fine actor: he gives a convincing performance. Plus, he must always have the last word!

Om is not a major accumulator or collector. Indeed, he has quite basic needs and wants. Ironically, he is not a major film buff either. Having had an overdose of films at the FTII and various film festivals earlier on, he can survive without visiting a theatre for years together. And apart from a few, he rarely watches his own films.

As for reading, Om may read a play once in a while but you will rarely catch him reading fiction or a thriller. One of the few fictional works he has enjoyed is Irving Wallace's *Lust for Life*. Since his surgery, though, he has been reading a lot of self-help books. When I gifted

Facing page: A wonderful sketch of Om Puri as his wife, Nandita sees him.

him Eknath Easwaran's *Take Your Time*, he was instantly hooked. He later read many more books by Easwaran and has gifted them to friends and also introduced me to *Climbing the Blue Mountain*, *Strength in the Storm*, among others. Perhaps Easwaran's uncomplicated philosophy appeals to Om's simpler side. And since Om is not overtly religious or ritualistic, he takes solace in spiritual reading.

While Om is not ritualistic, he does not mind others being so. Ours is a secular house and though I say my daily prayers, Om does not advertise his conversations with God. For example, instead of making a ritualistic hue and cry on his father's death anniversary, he quietly gives money to four or five elderly people in Bauji's memory. But once in a while, he does give in to superstitious people. Like the other day, I caught him giving a five-hundred-rupee note to the sweeper woman out of the blue as someone had advised him to do it on account of some eclipse! At such times favour-seekers easily cash in on his gullibility.

Om's wedding on May Day in Worli. From left to right: The marriage was solemnized in an Arya Samaj temple; the couple's friend, Chitra (left) and Govind Nihalani (right) looks on as the pandit completes the ceremony; celebrating their honeymoon at the Hollywood Walk of Fame in 1993.

Similarly, since Om is very open to ideas, he can get swayed by people easily. Especially over politics. He has neither been politically savvy nor had any overt political leanings. Some years ago, a few of his older friends who were communist sympathizers suddenly began to support the non-secular BJP. Never one to take politics seriously, Om got roped into campaigning for the New Delhi BJP candidate Vijay Goel during the 2001 elections for a lakh of rupees. When the BJP was routed, Om realized his stupidity and felt embarrassed. He quickly gave away the one lakh rupees to charity. It was later due to the prodding of Kapil Sibal and a few other sensible friends that Om formally joined the Congress party in 2004. Even after joining the Congress, he has preferred to remain on the sidelines.

Om usually relaxes by cooking, at times by gardening. These are his stress busters. He was first fascinated by cooking while watching his mother prepare those rare delights of his childhood. Later as a Boy Scout and living on his own since a very young age, he could rustle up

Jackie came to be called *bhaiya* (elder brother) when Ishaan grew up; here he is yet a babe-in-arms.

a meal at short notice. After a long day's shoot, Om comes and peeps into the kitchen. Even chopping vegetables over a couple of drinks is relaxing for him. Many a time I have caught him making *parathas* and relishing them with dollops of butter in the dead of the night.

When shooting abroad, Om insists on an apartment and loves to do grocery shopping. While I tend to get excited at the sight of pretty shop windows, Om salivates at the sight of colourful fruits and vegetables. He prefers the Indian variety in food but likes to experiment with recipes. More than being a gourmet cook, he excels at improvisation. I call him a 'food fixer'. Whenever I goof up a dish, he is easily able to do something to make it edible.

Om loves to call friends home and cook for them. And during his shoots abroad, his favourite pastime is to cook a meal for his co-stars and unit members. Though his favourite cuisines are Thai and Mexican, he cooks the Indian fare, like *pulaos*, *parathas* and *alu-palak raita*, among other dishes, quite well. One evening, he was cooking for Roland Joffe at his Bel Air residence that overlooked the entire Beverly Hills. When Om was kneading the dough for *rotis* (or chapatis), he realized there was no *belan* or rolling pin to roll the *rotis* with. He immediately took an empty wine bottle as his *belan* and sitting in Bel Air we had home-made fluffy *rotis* with delicious Indian curry.

On a boat ride during their second marriage anniversary in Seychelles.

A typical day in the life of Om Puri is to rise early, at the crack of dawn. At five he heads out for a walk at the Nana-Nani Park in front of the house. Then after two cups of tea he shaves, bathes and gets ready to head out for a shoot. He usually has a light breakfast of either fruits or two boiled egg whites. If he is home by 6 or 6.30 p.m., he heads to the nearby club for a swim. Back home it is a couple of drinks, a cuddle with Ishaan, an early dinner, a page or two of Easwaran and in bed by 10 p.m. Om hardly watches TV and just skims through the headlines on news channels.

The best time both of us have is usually over Om's customary two pegs, when he and I chat about all manner of things, concerning politics, literature, films, music, and wherever else the mood takes us. Om listens to me mesmerized as I talk about varied topics from scientific theories to Beethoven and I have realized over the years that he is a quick learner. And when Om decides to hold forth on any subject, one knows he talks with deep knowledge and understanding. Once he had pointed out that while he is 'deeply informed', I am 'widely read'. Quite a few of my views and opinions on films, particularly on Indian cinema, are due to his influence. In fact, many times, when he reads my columns he feels it is his thoughts that are being aired. I owe a lot of the maturity in my columns to these pre- and post-dinnertime conversations with Om, which I cherish greatly.

On a non-working day too, he rises early and goes for his walk; but he skips the grooming bit and heads out to the friendly neighbourhood *udipi*, Swadesh, where he enjoys a *sada dosa* and *chai* while he chats up with the other male buddies who are regulars there. Back home, he either potters with the plants or in the kitchen or generally chews on my brains. Since on his off-days he likes to be choosy about brushing his teeth or taking a bath, we have to put up with his unkempt look about the house. On days like these he likes to discipline Ishaan or haul me up, albeit mildly – not letting it escape us who the boss is. In case we forgot!

After a lazy lunch at home and a nap followed by a swim in the evening, he either calls a couple of friends to sample his culinary skills or goes to the Pahwas' place for dinner. Manoj and Seema Pahwa treat him like an elder brother. They say, 'His simplicity, especially when he saunters into our home at short notice and shares our meals, is very endearing.'

Sometimes, we also head out to one of the nearby eateries. Om does not like travelling too much for a meal. 'Choose a place within half a kilometre from the house,' is the option he gives us. So it is Legacy of China for Chinese, Pop Tate's for Continental, Satranj Napoli for Italian or Urban Tadka for good ole Punjabi cuisine. Earlier, Om abhorred eating out, but nowadays he has begun to enjoy it, thanks mainly to me.

These days we joke about the changing times. We decide on a fancy place, the cuisine and the cost it will incur. Then we decide to eat at home instead and pat ourselves for having managed to save money – especially at the time of recession!

Facing page: On the beach with Nandita and Ishaan in Zurich.

However, he still hates clubbing and late night parties. Any invite that says '9 p.m. onwards' is relegated to the bin.

~

Having grown up in his maternal uncles' family of farmers, Om was always lured by land. He often jokes that had he not been an actor he would have either been a cook or a farmer. And he keeps saying he would like to retire to a farm. It was twenty years ago that Om had decided to look for an ideal farmhouse. His ex-secretary Dubeyji took him to see many plots in Maharashtra. Finally, six years ago Om zeroed in on his ideal weekend getaway in Khandala, close to the Deccan Hills area.

The bungalow in question was bought from one Mansoorbhai with a beautiful garden, which the previous owners had landscaped into three layers, the topmost overlooking the Western Ghats. Om named it 'Ishaan Kutir' meaning Ishaan's hut. In front of the bungalow Om bought a small plot of land, called 'Ishaan Vatika' (Ishaan Garden), where he lets his farming creativity flow. From *makai* (sweet corn) to brinjals and papayas, and bananas to alphonso mangoes, our 'mini farm' yields nearly everything. The thrill of eating homegrown vegetables and fruits has a different flavour altogether. We try to head out there on Friday evenings and return by Sunday evening. Those two days in Khandala are enough to rejuvenate us for the rest of the week.

Lonavala and Khandala used to have a lot of Parsi population. Some of the old bungalows are still there, albeit dilapidated. Yet, the town retains its old charm without a single mall or multiplex (I hear one is going to come up soon though) and is famous for its fudges and *chikkis* (sticky, sweet jaggery and peanut candies). Buying groceries in the local market, walking around the hills, visiting neighbours for a cuppa and generally catching up on sleep are the things to enjoy there. And the best part is, as Om had always envisioned, we can reach this paradise in less than two hours from our doorstep. Sometimes it takes longer to reach downtown in Bombay!

~

'Husbands are street angels and house devils' – an old proverb. Many will agree with me. Flip the gender and it applies to both sexes.

Nandita characteristically holds the phone to Om's ear on the occasion of receiving the OBE honour.

I have a short fuse, which snaps every now and then. Om has one which when it snaps, booms the neighbourhood down. Some years back, a friend had called and asked whether Om and I had had a huge fight in the morning. I was surprised as she lives a good kilometre away from us. 'Yes. But how the hell do you know?' I asked.

'Oh. Mom told me,' was her reply.

Her mother lives on the third floor in the same building as ours and she heard Om's voice booming all the way down four floors!

During the initial years of our marriage, Om was wary about parting with his money. He would never give me a monthly allowance for household expenditure and preferred to pay the bills personally. He would be away for months and the milkman or grocer would be knocking for their dues, every time to be told, '*Saab* is away.' Once when I complained to a friend, Om's simple logic was, 'What if she runs away with my money?' It was only after a couple of years that Om loosened his purse strings and tightened his trust towards me.

One instance of his simple generosity was taking my mother to London during the filming of *My Son The Fanatic.* It was Om's way of making upto Bauji whom he could not even take out on a flight, leave alone abroad, during his lean years.

And yet Om, like most men, has a habit of keeping a tab on how much he spends on his woman. Once after a heated argument, Om decided to gift me (a little grudgingly though) a Cartier Tank Francaise (knowing my penchant for watches). Since it was quite expensive, I told him he need not buy it. Om magnanimously claimed, 'No. Now that I have made up my mind, I will. Besides, it is for my wife.' I was touched. But whenever we have a showdown, he doesn't forget to remind me of the fortune he spent on the watch!

Om also suffers from selective memory. He loves to remember what he wants and obliterates the rest. Once when we went to Park Hotel in Kolkata after two years and got the same room. I reminded him but he feigned ignorance. But of course he had not forgotten the huge telephone bill I had run up on the last occasion!

Om by nature is simple. He does not believe in brands so much so that his favourite watch brand is Titan. (Only recently has he started sporting an Armani since Naseer gave him one on his last birthday.) 'I would rather spend on health and education than drive a Mercedes or BMW even if I can afford one.' Similarly, on his birthday, he would prefer someone to give him socks or a hairbrush than a bottle of expensive perfume or shades.

Whenever we travel, within the country or abroad, Om provides us with the best. But at the end of each trip he calculates the entire cost of food, travel and stay and tells me, 'Hey look! I spent this amount on you.' Initially, I used to get upset. But I have learnt over time that it is his middle-class nature and will never change. I have even got wiser. I tell him back, 'Listen, let's divide the entire expenses into three. You've spent only a third on me. The rest is on yourself and your son.' He then gives me a sheepish smile. These little quirks make him so human, so endearing.

But Om tends to have a unidimensional view of suffering. For him only the economically poor suffer, the rich do not. The other day,

Relaxing over drinks with Naseer at home, dressed in a kimono.

while reading *A Princess Remembers*, the memoirs of Gayatri Devi, I remarked what a fascinating read it made.

'But what was so fascinating about her life? She was rich. She did not have to suffer. There was no struggle,' came the retort.

I did not argue. I know Om loves empathizing with the underdog and not particularly with the master.

Although he has received the OBE for his contribution to English cinema, his language and accent both remain true to his Punjabi roots. Despite years of trying to make him pronounce 'October' correctly, he still says 'Ak-too-ber'.

Once during an argument, I exclaimed, 'Zilch!'

He interrupted the argument and asked me suspiciously, 'What is zilch?'

'Zero.'

'So why can't you say zero? Why use complicated words?'

A few years later, I met the legendary actress Zohra Sehgal. She had worked with Om in *The Mystic Masseur* in Trinidad. I introduced myself as Om's wife. She immediately asked, 'The zilch-*wali*?'

That's the extent of Om's wonderment at new English words!

I too have had my embarrassing moments with Hindi. It has now improved by leaps and bounds thanks to Om. During my early days in Bombay, someone had called one afternoon and Om did not want to talk at the time. So he gestured to me to tell him he was asleep. In my most polite tone, I told the person, 'Omji *so rahi hai*.' Om nearly collapsed out of shock. He wanted to burst out right then but had to maintain his silence. Surprised, when I asked him about his reaction, he replied, 'God! You changed my gender!'

Talking about gender, there are certain notions about work that have not changed for him despite having seen a different life. 'What do you do the whole day? Nothing. Just write a few columns here and there' is a typical salvo he fires at me during our typical arguments.

'Well, I run the house, look after my son apart from writing the few columns here and there!' Not to be outdone, I retaliate.

'But aren't there servants to cook and clean? So what do you do?'

'Well, I tell them how to clean and what to cook,' I reply, exasperated. Om still thinks I should physically get down to cleaning and cooking or else it doesn't count as work!

Once, journalist Alpana Chowdhury while interviewing us, asked me, 'Is he a typical chauvinist?' Since Om was sitting next to me, I looked about a bit uncomfortably trying to frame my answer as diplomatically as possible.

'Well, err …'

'I'll answer that for her,' he said seeing my discomfiture. 'You see, I am very liberal. I don't mind my wife wearing jeans and I don't expect her to carry a *thaili* (cloth bag) and go buy vegetables in the market …'

'Well, the very fact that your image of a woman is that of carrying a *thaili* and buying vegetables, shows you have very chauvinistic ideas about them,' Alpana interrupted. Being caught off-guard, Om looked a little uncomfortable, switched the tape off and told Alpana,

'I'm shooting tomorrow at Filmistan. Drop by there for the rest of the interview.'

Alpana and I have a good laugh whenever we recollect this.

Another time, we had a part-time maid who would come at seven sharp in the morning. Being a mild insomniac, I tend to go into a deep sleep in the early hours of the morning. Once when the maid rang the bell, Om woke me up and told me, 'The bell's ringing. Go open the door.' I sauntered groggily and came back and flopped myself back on the bed. Suddenly, I saw Om grinning.

'What are you laughing at? And why did you not open the door yourself? You were awake. Why did you have to wake me up?' I asked, irritable.

'Wifely duties you see,' he smiled smugly.

In fact, part of the reason for my insomnia is Om's talent for snoring the house down. Sometimes, I lie awake for the better part of the night, listening intently to the variations in his snoring. I honestly feel I can record a classical disc with all the different movements!

Now, having got used to it, I sometimes miss it when he is not around, albeit happily.

There are times when I wake him up to tell him to stop snoring. At such times, he apologizes and promptly goes back to sleep – and to snoring.

Sometimes, he himself wakes up and asks confusedly, 'Was I snoring? I heard myself.'

~

On the first of May 2008, it was our fifteenth wedding anniversary. Om, who does not believe in parties or celebrations, personally called up a hundred close friends at a well-known suburban diner and celebrated with music, food and drinks. Of course, he held the party on 30 April to bring in the first of May, as it is a dry day in Maharashtra!

# His Son's Father

Just like every woman yearns for motherhood at some point of time in her life, every man yearns for fatherhood. Even though he may have a macho self-image.

Om was never overtly fond of children and he hardly has much patience with them. He enjoyed playing with his friends' children, especially Pradeep and Veena Upoor's son, Chinu, but that was the most he could handle. In small doses. But there came a point when he felt he needed to have a family of his own once his nephews had flown the coop. When his son, Ishaan was born in 1997, Om embraced his newfound fatherhood, though a bit apprehensively. A few months later, his paternal urges took over and he began to enjoy himself.

Ishaan was in a tearing hurry to enter the world. Though he was due sometime in the middle of October, I burst my waterbag suddenly and Ishaan was born on the 2nd of July, nearly three months premature. The first few weeks were crucial for the little fellow. He barely weighed two pounds – only 950 grams! The tiny thing spent the next three months battling all odds to reach an ideal weight. During this time, his lungs had to be artificially injected with surfactant injections that Om had to personally acquire as they were not only expensive, but not easily available too. Similarly, Ishaan got plasma one night when the doctors called Om urgently asking for blood. His shoots had to be cancelled at short notice. Those days he was filming *China Gate* and Naseer, Danny Denzongpa, Amrish Puri and others willingly adjusted their dates.

Like father, like son. Ishaan is a survivor. Om was amazed at the way the pocket-sized baby fought to live. He wanted to name him Vir:

Facing page: Ishaan and Om in a playful mood in Zurich.

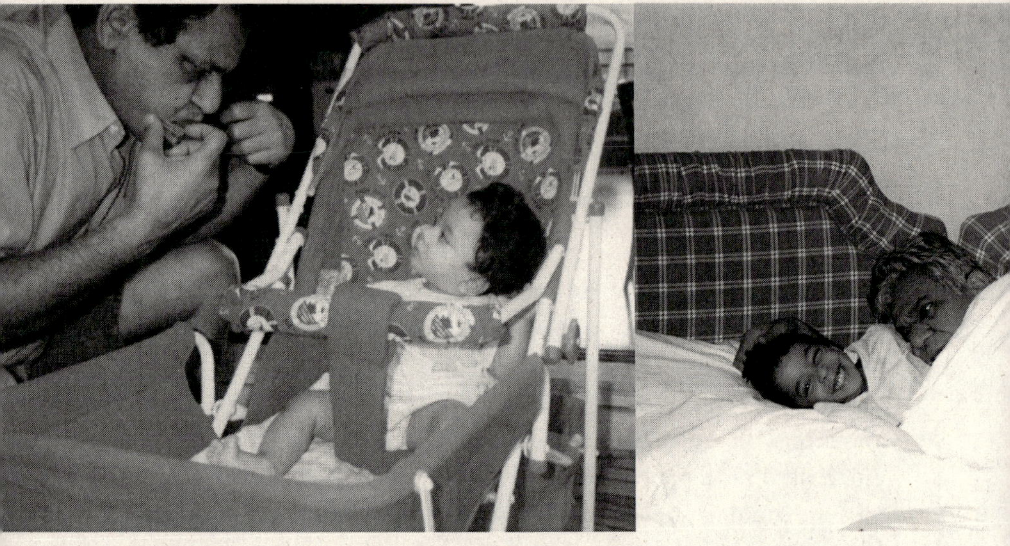

Left to right: Om the father playing to Ishaan's tunes when he was around ten to twelve months old; trying to put the naughty four-year-old to sleep in England; having fun in the tub with Ishaan, just three years old at the time, in London.

brave. 'Vir Puri will sound more like *bhel puri, paani puri.* He'll be made fun of at school. Why don't we call him Ishaan, which means the north-east or the first ray of the sun in Sanskrit and God's blessing in Arabic,' I urged. This time Om did not argue. And that is how Ishaan Vir Puri was named.

When Ishaan was undergoing the routine tests mainly done on premature babies, he was found with ROP 5 in his left eye. In layman terms, virtually blind in one eye. We both were devastated. On reaching home, Om sat on the terrace and howled. The first he had done in several decades. I, on the other hand, who was wont to burst into tears for little things, was stoic in my grief. 'We will do our best,' I told Om.

'Some years ago, when Ishaan was a baby, I was driving up to Ooty. It was early morning and the first rays of the sun were lightly kissing the trees and flowers. It was a beautiful sight. I remembered Ishaan's disability and my eyes blurred with tears. I prayed that he is able to appreciate such sights later on in life.

'Today I am very proud of him. He is bright and always full of

questions. He is among the top three rankers in his class and recently even won a silver and a bronze medal in sports. Friends and teachers adore him and he never embarrasses me. He has the memory of an elephant and is very systematic when it comes to his books and toys. You will never see them littered about the house.'

Fatherhood had come late for Om and at times his energy levels were much lower than other young fathers. Nevertheless, he always gave his best shot. Despite his hectic schedules and frequent travels, Om did manage to spend a lot of time with Ishaan and even did the occasional duty of nappy-changing and walking the baby to sleep.

Though in Om's case, it was more like driving. There would be nights when after a hard day's shoot, just at Om's time to retire, Ishaan would bawl the house down with his gripe pains. So in the middle of the night, Om would be driving around Mount Mary or Juhu, nearly dozing off at the wheels while I tried to rock Ishaan to sleep.

But the onus of bringing up Ishaan was largely mine, one that I took on with alacrity. And the wonderful help I had in the initial years with a paediatric nurse, Sister Victoria, was indispensable. She became a family member to us in no time.

Since Om loves to have his family around during his shoots, Ishaan

Left to right: Om plays with eight-month-old Ishaan; with Ishaan in England; Ishaan monkeys around with his father in Monte Carlo; Ishaan gulps down the ice cream being offered by his father at Locarno.

is a well-travelled child. From sharing a pizza with Tom Hanks to having dinner with Prince Albert of Monaco, Ishaan has been around. At his age, Om's luxury was a sweet biscuit!

Om reminisces, 'I remember on his first trip to London during the filming of *East is East*, he was barely a year old and was wrapped up in his pram with only his face exposed. Every now and then I would rub my palms hard and place them on his cheeks. His face would brighten up and he would give a gleeful smile.

'When Ishaan was a baby, I enjoyed shopping for him on my various trips. I would specially pick up educational toys from Early Learning Centre. Even now I try to get him local toys from various countries and local musical instruments.

'He continues to be outgoing. Once during the shoot of *Dev*, he came to the sets. Since I was in the shot, he promptly went to Amitabh Bachchan's (whom he considers his buddy) vanity van and chatted him up for a while. Recently, on meeting the Pakistani singer, Farida Khanum, he immediately broke into a raga for her when she asked him to sing. And this was before a roomful of at least sixty to seventy

people. He is not self-conscious at all. At his age, it was a different story for me.'

Om finds himself at a loss for words when at times Ishaan questions him why he cannot play cricket or football and other rough games. Or why he has to wear spectacles while other children don't. Or why he is not as big or as tall like the other boys his age.

'His enthusiasm is amazing,' Om says. 'At such times I encourage him to play table tennis or learn swimming. He is learning music and loves to paint. For years, as a little child, Ishaan wanted to become a pilot. Now he wants to become an actor. Once his mother jokingly asked him, "So you want to be a hero?"

'"No. I want to be a good character actor like Baba." It was one of the proudest moments of my life!

'His concern for me also extends to the days I am tired. He gives me a massage and pedicure with his little hands. As a father I try to give him as much exposure as possible. Later, it is up to him to choose. I can only guide and advise him,' concludes Om.

## MY FATHER, MY BABA

My father is Om Puri, the very famous actor. He acted in many films like *Hera Pheri, Jane Bhi Do Yaaro, Tamas, Gandhi, Wolf* and many more. I call him Baba.

He is 58 years old. He is a great actor and I am very proud of him.

When my father was small, he was very poor. But he is now what he is today because of his hard work and education. He took me to many places like London, New York, Los Angeles, Prague and many more. Last year he took me to Malaysia, Singapore, USA, France, Canada and Monaco.

He is very kind to me and he cares for me and he loves me and he does the best for me. But I don't like my father yelling at my mother or being rude to her. I get angry with him then.

I also don't like my father to smoke. So I told him not to smoke many times. But he did not listen. Then I took the cigarette packet and threw it from the seventh floor. But then he went down and brought it back. Then I took out the cigarettes and threw them one by one from the seventh floor and kept the empty packet where it was for him. But no, again he went down and got it back. Then I got angry and crushed it and threw it in the dustbin. For years I kept doing this and my father kept on scolding me for this small thing. On my birthday he told me that he will try to stop smoking but today he does a lot of smoking.

One of the best moments I remember was in London. I was small and staying with my father and mother in The Dorchester. Then in the middle of the night there was a fire alarm. My father quickly took a towel and picked me up from the bed and wrapped me in it. He carried me and ran down. But later they told us it was a false alarm.

In London I remember going to Sainsbury's early in the mornings with my father to buy things. Then my father would take me to a very lovely garden called Kensington Garden where he made me feed ducks, squirrels, birds. The birds also sat on our hands. Then we went back to the apartment to surprise my mother. I also enjoyed my trip to Legoland. My father and me tried most of the rides.

I enjoy the 6.30 a.m. walks in the mornings with my father in the Nana-Nani Park in front of our house. At 7.30 a.m., me and my father have juice from the juice-*walla* near Nana-Nani Park.

My father always likes to hug and sleep with me. But when he goes to sleep, I pull away as he snores very loudly. I call him Kharrate King in fun. *Kharrate* in Hindi means snoring. Another thing I get irritated with my father is when he is not shooting and stays home. He never has a bath or changes his clothes or shaves. My mother and me keep telling him but he ignores.

But when he goes for shootings, he has a bath and goes well-dressed. And sometimes when he is home, he can be very boring with us. But other times he can be very cheerful and full of fun.

Whenever I speak good English and use difficult English words he says, '*Oye,* Ma *ki poonch*. You pick up these words from your mother.' My father teaches me to speak good Hindi as his Hindi is very good. He also teaches me to use some Urdu words in my Hindi. We both play a Hindi-Urdu word game so that my Hindi becomes better. Whenever I use difficult Hindi words, my mother says, '*Baap ka chamcha*.'

He gets me nice toys from all over the world. He is very kind to me. He is a very good father and takes a lot of care. He is a true father and the best father in the whole world.

*(This essay was written in the first person by Ishaan as part of his school essay in 2008. Apart from correcting spelling errors and punctuating the piece, I have let the words and language remain his.)*

Young Ishaan's pencil portrait of Om.

Om was a jury member at the Monte Carlo film festival in 2006. The rest of the jury also includes Prince Albert of Moncao (fifth from right).

Above: A still from *Dev* (2004) on the cover of *Screen*, where director Govind Nihalani brought the two great actors, Om Puri and Amitabh Bachchan, together for the first time.

Right: A poster from Ismail Merchant's *In Custody* (1994), based on Anita Desai's novel and script.

# Overview of Indian Cinema

Om Puri

When I first came to Bombay in 1976 to join the Hindi film industry, I had behind me an NSD and FTII background. NSD's impact had been much deeper. Unfortunately, the Hindi film industry as a whole does not recognize talent without glamour attached to it. Here, actors with good looks and glamour are most welcome, as also are actors with glamour and talent, and more than anything, actors with glamour and family connections, never mind the talent bit. Bollywood is a feudal system, hierarchical. While a star can command ten crore rupees for a film, a character actor in the same film will not get more than fifty lakhs and a spot boy at the bottom of the ladder would get five hundred rupees a day. The disparity is glaring.

It has been a roller coaster ride for me, with both the highs and lows in equal measure. Maybe I have been one of the lucky few considering my background.

In the mid-seventies, when the wave of change was carrying all of us with it, we saw cinema, theatre or television as means of making a difference. We were very aware that commercial cinema was not part of this scheme. It was (and still is) an entertainer devoid of social responsibility. In this sense, we knew Indian commercial cinema to be escapist. Even when it played around with real-life situations, its characters were two-dimensional, black or white, with no shades of grey. The onus of destroying 'evil' and restoring order and goodness fell on the virtuous 'hero' of the film, thus absolving the audience of their own social responsibility and making them complacent. The vague category of 'character actors' was brought in to affect some kind of balance and give a feel of real life.

As a new entrant, I was motivated by the middle cinema of Bimal Roy, V. Shantaram, Hrishikesh Mukherjee, Basu Chatterjee, Gulzar and others and in some measure the art house cinema of Satyajit Ray, Mrinal Sen, Shyam Benegal and their ilk. Slowly, the contradiction in me grew. The trouble was that middle Indian cinema would not accept actors like me as they had their established stars like Amol Palekar, Sanjeev Kumar, even Amitabh Bachchan sometimes, and others, though these films were commercially viable. And art films were usually low-budget films and our pay couldn't really compare to that of actors in the other genres. It was like surviving on bread alone – without butter or jam.

So I was left with the choice to do bit roles in commercial films for financial sustenance. Though I did try to resist commercial cinema for quite some time, I succumbed to it finally as money was equally important as art. Some of my colleagues from 'art cinema' commented on this shift but I have always maintained that I do not really discriminate between the two genres. One just cannot earmark a film as merely art or commercial. The choice is between a good or a bad film.

But as an artist, I never compromised on what I had to do on-screen, even if the film was not up to the standard. Some films are in fact remembered only for their bit roles and gradually I was recognized in that sphere. It did not give me total fulfilment, a satisfaction of the mind and heart, but a niche did get created within commercial cinema for meaningful character roles and actors at the fringes. However, one encouraging factor was that the shelf life of a star is often limited, which is not the case with character roles.

I also worked in British films and television for a while that helps me compare the two industries. The British film industry is tiny compared to the Indian film industry. It was only after films like *The Full Monty, East is East* and *Bend it like Beckham*, that Hollywood and the big worldwide players took notice of it. But to an average Indian, any film with white actors is a 'Hollywood film', even if it is from Portugal or France or Germany or even China. With the increasing number of English films I did, people here assumed that 'Om Puri was making pots of money doing Hollywood films'. On the contrary,

I would have made much more had I stuck only to Subhash Ghai's or David Dhawan's films here.

The main criterion for me to work extensively in England, among others, was a crucial one: work discipline. There was complete lack of discipline in Bollywood that demoralized trained actors like myself and by the late '90s, we did not even have the support of the better organized parallel film fraternity. So as Naseer retreated into theatre, I found solace in English cinema and television.

After that experience, I can see even more clearly, the way things are meted out in this industry. I rage within at the outrageously feudal setup. In the early years too, talented actors were not given their due as roles were written with the leading heroes in mind. So I thought, maybe in my old age, when I would have proved my mettle, I would get to play select character roles. But ironically, today, most of the good character roles (*Sarkar, Khakee*, for instance) go to the yesteryear stars.

The latest trend in Bollywood is that second- and third-generation filmmakers and actors are busy promoting their own children. The struggle for a talented actor who does not come from a family with a background in films is much harder than those belonging to star families, even though he is good-looking. And particularly for women without a film background, it is even harder and they sometimes have to pay a steep price for stardom.

Even so, some professionalism has seeped into the industry recently, like a bound script, call sheets, coming to the sets on time and qualified technicians. The so-called 'black' or unaccounted money that was basically the money laundered from the underworld and builders has virtually gone. With the gradual corporatization of the industry, legitimate 'white' money has taken over.

And it is in this great Indian film industry where there is harmony among the various communities. Where Hindus, Muslims and Christians, all break bread together. Where a communal clash at a shoot is unheard of. May it always stay this way.

# Tips to Actors

## Om Puri

These notes were taken down by Nandita during an interaction I had with students at Whistling Woods, Mumbai, in April 2008. I was invited by Naseeruddin Shah, who heads the Acting Department there. These notes may help aspiring actors understand the medium and also the problems they might encounter during the course of their fledgling years.

**Observation**: This is perhaps one of the most important tools for an actor. Not only does an actor need to observe and notice his surroundings, he has to take a deep interest in what he observes. As a child, I would often go to the marketplace or the railway station and observe people and their movements and mannerisms.

By observation, I imply feelings and imaginations as well. Even reading newspapers or hearing the radio sharpens those senses. For instance, soon after the Latur earthquake the story of a little boy moved me deeply. He had lost his entire family in the calamity but refused to cry for many days till one day he saw his domestic cow. He hugged it and howled. I tried to imagine his emotions and I could feel the tragedy as mine.

**Intellect and Instinct**: Though they are very different, these two primary abilities go hand in hand. To be a good actor you need to be well-read and well-informed, while acting spontaneously.

**Involvement and Detachment**: It is of utmost importance to be totally involved as an actor, yet there has to be a kind of detachment. A good actor is one who will be objective about his character without losing his passion. Only passion will make you an indulgent performer. For example, while Waheeda Rehman excelled in drama, Meena Kumari excelled in melodrama.

Take a situation in a scene when you get a phone call informing you of your brother's death,

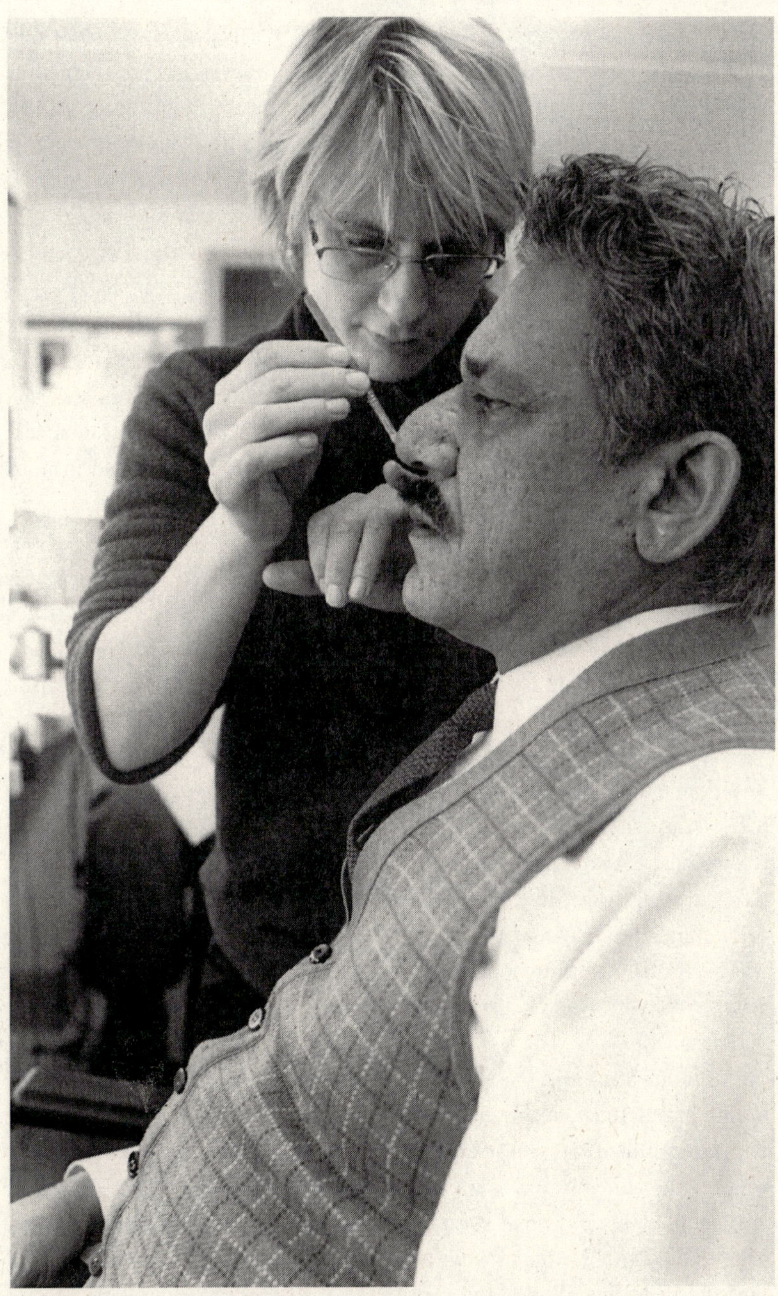

Om getting makeup done for his role as the Pakistani patriarch in the award-winning film, *East is East*.

Rehearsing for a Kabuki performance in Japan with Shabana Azmi.

think what the character would really do. If he is a nervy person, he may rush out in panic or start howling, if not, he may simply put his wallet and keys in his pocket, lock the door and head out, while intensifying the emotion through the face not through exaggerated bodily gestures.

**Subtext**: An actor enacts according to his script, but how well he enacts his role cannot be based on his reading of the text alone. There is a subtext to everything, the 'between the lines', which is instrumental in moulding an actor's sensibilities for a well-rounded performance.

While preparing for a role, you have to find out more about the character. For example, there is a scene in the text where a young man walks to the bus stop to meet his girlfriend, wearing jeans and a *kurta*. Now your work on the subtext begins. Why is the man walking; does he not have enough money to take an auto or taxi; then maybe he is either unemployed or he lives in a small PG dig or with his family in cramped quarters; wearing a jeans with *kurta* may also signify his ideological or political leanings – he may be a Marxist or an activist; not being too well-off, he probably would have had a modest breakfast or maybe just a cup of tea, etc. All these thoughts will help prepare and enrich your performance. You can of course also ask the writer what he had in mind about this character.

**Inspiration**: Be only inspired by great performances or performers, do not imitate them. Inspiration is more of an ideal, a standard to look up to, not an example of how to act.

**Representation**: As an actor most of the time we are representing a character instead of being one. Like in *Charlie Wilson's War*, I was merely representing Zia-ul Haq and not being Zia. As an actor, sometimes you merely look at a character and replay it.

**Being a Character**: However, the ultimate bliss of acting is being the character. When you totally identify with the character and believe in it, then you become the character. Some examples of the films in which I became the character are *Aakrosh*, *Ardh Satya*, *Susman* and *City Of Joy.*

But despite all efforts, at times you are not able to 'be' a character throughout, so you end up representing as well as being – or a combination of both.

**Length and Breadth of Roles**: In order to make your mark and then survive in the exclusive world of acting on screen, you have to be careful what you pick and what you don't. You may or may not get the lead role in a big or important project, in television or in cinema. At that time, your decision to accept or reject a role being offered to you can make all the difference in your career. Here are some examples of roles usually underestimated by new actors:

*Cameos*: Doing a cameo depends on the importance of the role. If it is a crucial or pivotal scene to the film or it is with a well-known director or part of a prestigious project, you should do it.

*Short Appearances*: Learn to recognize and accept your abilities. If you know you do not possess the looks of a hero, go for character roles; if you do not have the body of an action hero, go ahead and check out your flair for comedy; turn your drawbacks into advantages. Do not shy away from any medium, be it films, television, theatre, et al. And for God's sake, do not wait for the 'magnum opus'!

**Is Training Necessary for an Actor?** There are instances of great actors who have managed well without any formal training in acting. But I say "yes", training is necessary for an actor.We are all born with a talent, be it acting, singing, painting or writing. Training helps you enhance that talent. As an actor with training, you can liberate yourself. By this I mean if the script or a particular director is weak, you can contribute to the strength of the film. Training helps you develop a scientific approach to your character. Like in *Singh is Kinng* I added a lot of impromptu dialogues in Punjabi so that the Punjabi humour comes out loud. Similarly I have also contributed my little bit to even Ray's *Sadgati* and Vishal Bharadwaj's *Maqbool*. (See instances in Let's Go to the Movies)

**How to Prepare for a Role:** First consider the script to be your Bible and like you read the Bible or the Bhagvad Gita over and over again, similarly get your script under your skin.This will help you bring out the subtext in the script.

The physicality in a role is important. If your body is not suited to a particular character then you have to work on it. Like Robert Di Nero put on weight in *Raging Bull*. Similarly, I went on a diet as well as swam vigorously to lose weight in *City of Joy* where I play a rickshaw-puller. And a rickshaw-puller demands a lean look because he pulls a rickshaw atleast for eight to ten hours a day. Physicality also means learning the skills of your character you will be portraying onscreen to be comfortable with your role. In *Susman* I learnt to weave as I play a weaver. Similarly in *City of Joy* I learnt to pull a rickshaw as I play a rickshaw-puller.

Apart from physical preparedness, mental awareness is essential. It is very important for an actor apart from observing and thinking, to keep in touch with progressing reality, his surroundings and be socially and politically aware. Another important source of this awareness is by interacting with people. Sometimes even animals. According to Ebrahim Alkazi, "learn acting from animals and children as they have no inhibitions." To essay the role of a bohemian in one of my earliest films *Shayyad*, my main inspiration was a goat in a crowded marketplace in Indore! The goat kept running from one vegetable kiosk to another and inspite of being shooed away, remained unfazed. And that was my character in the film.

**Co-workers**: In an industry where more things are accomplished through an interpersonal rapport, than through the professional route, you need to be careful how you interact without compromising your goals. Even if you do not like a certain project, never reject a producer harshly. Be polite. You never know when you might need the same producer again.

Secondly, always respect a director's ideas, and even if you disagree with him try and come to a decision that seems mutual. Because no matter what, he is the captain of the ship and you signed with him as your director. Finally, co-actors are the people you will be socializing with regularly and it is important to respect each one. After all, acting is a symphony orchestra, where each plays a different instrument to the best of his ability so that all sounds harmonize beautifully.

Make the best of the situation because a project is bigger than just your role.

# Om Puri: A Filmography

Om Puri has worked in over 200 hundred Indian films in various roles and nearly 30-odd international films under directors of national and international repute. Since it is not possible to list all the films, here are some major films of his long career in cinema.

| INDIAN FILMS | DIRECTOR | YEAR |
|---|---|---|
| Chor Chor Chhup Jaaye | B.V. Karanth | 1975 |
| Shayyad | Madan Bavaria | 1979 |
| Godhuli | Girish Karnad & B.V. Karanth | 1979 |
| Shodh | Biplab Roy Chowdhury | 1980 |
| Jaane Bhi Do Yaaro | Kundan Shah | 1981 |
| Arohan | Shyam Benegal | 1981 |
| Aakrosh | Govind Nihalani | 1982 |
| Ardh Satya | Govind Nihalani | 1984 |
| Bhavni Bhavai | Ketan Mehta | 1984 |
| Chokh | Utpalendu Chakraborty | 1985 |
| Sparsh | Sai Paranjpe | 1985 |
| Aghaat | Govind Nihalani | 1986 |
| Tamas | Govind Nihalani | 1986 |
| Susman | Shyam Benegal | 1988 |
| Mirch Masala | Ketan Mehta | 1988 |
| Sadgati | Satyajit Ray | 1988 |
| Genesis | Mrinal Sen | 1990 |
| Dharavi | Sudhir Misra | 1992 |
| Patang | Goutam Ghose | 1993 |
| Ghayal | Rajkumar Santoshi | 1993 |
| Target | Sandip Ray | 1994 |
| Raath | Ram Gopal Varma | 1994 |
| Droh Kaal | Govind Nihalani | 1994 |
| Prem Granth | Rajiv Kapoor | 1994 |
| Aastha | Basu Bahttacharya | 1995 |
| Pyar To Hona Hi Tha | Anees Bazmi | 1995 |

| | | |
|---|---|---|
| Gupt | Rajiv Rai | 1995 |
| Mrityudand | Prakash Jha | 1996 |
| Maachis | Gulzar | 1996 |
| Chachi 420 | Kamal Hasan | 1997 |
| China Gate | Rajkumar Santoshi | 1998 |
| Dulhan Hum Le Jayenge | David Dhawan | 1999 |
| Pukar | Rajkumar Santoshi | 1999 |
| Kunwara | David Dhawan | 2000 |
| Hera Pheri | Priyadarshan | 2000 |
| Kurukshetra | Mahesh Manjrekar | 2000 |
| Bollywood Calling | Nagesh Kukunoor | 2001 |
| AK-47 | Shivraj Kumar | 2001 |
| Aan | Madhur Bhandarkar | 2002 |
| Dhoop | Ashwini Chowdhry | 2003 |
| Yuva | Mani Ratnam | 2003 |
| King of Bollywood | Piyush Jha | 2003 |
| Dev | Govind Nihalani | 2004 |
| Maqbool | Vishal Bharadwaj | 2004 |
| Malamaal Weekly | Priyadarshan | 2005 |
| Lakshya | Farhan Akhtar | 2005 |
| Rang De Basanti | Rakeysh Mehra | 2006 |
| Don | Farhan Akhtar | 2006 |
| Victoria 2003 | Ananth Mahadevan | 2007 |
| Budhdha Mar Gaya | Rahul Rawail | 2007 |
| Dhol | Priyadarshan | 2007 |
| Singh is Kinng | Anees Bazmi | 2008 |
| Dilli 6 | Rakeysh Mehra | 2009 |
| Billo Barber | Priyadarshan | 2009 |

On the anvil: A sequel to *East is East* called *West is West* to be shot at the end of 2009, Renzil D. Silva's *Kurban* and Vipul Shah's *Action Replay* among others.

| **INTERNATIONAL FILMS** | **DIRECTOR** | **YEAR** |
|---|---|---|
| Gandhi | Richard Attenborough | 1985 |
| Sam & Me | Deepa Mehta | 1990 |
| City of Joy | Roland Joffe | 1991 |
| Burning Season | Richard Harvey | 1992 |

| | | |
|---|---|---|
| Wolf | Mike Nichols | 1993 |
| In Custody | Ismail Merchant | 1993 |
| Brothers in Trouble | Udayan Prasad | 1995 |
| The Ghost and the Darkness | Steven Hopkins | 1996 |
| My Son the Fanatic | Udayan Prasad | 1998 |
| Such a Long Journey | Sturla Gunarson | 1998 |
| East is East | Damien O'Donnell | 1999 |
| The Zookeeper | Ralph Ziman | 2000 |
| Parole Officer | John Duigan | 2000 |
| Happy Now | Phillippa Cousins | 2001 |
| Code 46 | Michael Winterbottom | 2002 |
| Charlie Wilson's War | Mike Nichols | 2006 |
| Shoot on Sight | Jag Mundhra | 2007 |

**INDIAN TELEVISION**

| SERIAL | DIRECTOR | YEAR |
|---|---|---|
| Yatra (Journey) | Shyam Benegal | 1987 |
| Bharat Ek Khoj (Discovery Of India) | Shyam Benegal | 1988 |
| Mr Yogi | Ketan Mehta | 1988 |
| Kakaji Kahin (Where is Kakaji) | Basu Chatterjee | 1989 |
| Rishte (Relationships) | Hrishikesh Mukherjee | 1990 |
| Kirdar (Character) | Gulzar | 1993 |
| Sea Hawks | Anubhav Sinha | 1997 |
| Jasoos Vijay (Detective Vijay) | BBC Trust | 2002 |

**INTERNATIONAL TELEVISION**

| SERIAL | DIRECTOR | YEAR |
|---|---|---|
| The Jewel in the Crown | Christopher Morahan | 1982 |
| Murder | Beeban Kidron | 2001 |
| White Teeth | Julian Jarrold | 2002 |
| Second Generation | John Sen | 2003 |
| The Canterbury Tales | Kate Bartlett | 2004 |

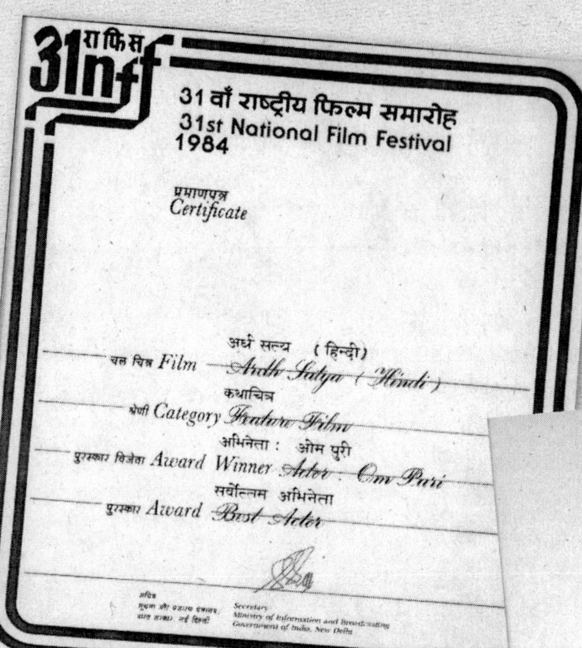

31 राफिस 31nff

31 वाँ राष्ट्रीय फिल्म समारोह
31st National Film Festival
1984

प्रमाणपत्र
Certificate

चल चित्र Film अर्ध सत्य (हिन्दी) Ardh Satya (Hindi)

श्रेणी Category कथाचित्र Feature Film

पुरस्कार विजेता Award Winner अभिनेता : ओम पुरी Actor : Om Puri

पुरस्कार Award सर्वोत्तम अभिनेता Best Actor

सचिव
सूचना और प्रसारण मंत्रालय,
भारत सरकार, नई दिल्ली

Secretary
Ministry of Information and Broadcasting
Government of India, New Delhi

The second National Award Om received for his outstanding performance in *Ardh Satya*.

Elizabeth R

**Elizabeth the Second,** by the Grace of God of the United Kingdom of Great Britain and Northern Ireland and of Her other Realms and Territories Queen, Head of the Commonwealth, Defender of the Faith and Sovereign of the Most Excellent Order of the British Empire to Om Puri

Greeting

**Whereas** We have thought fit to nominate and appoint you to be an Honorary Officer of the Civil Division of Our said Most Excellent Order of the British Empire

**We do** by these presents grant unto you the Dignity of an Honorary Officer of Our said Order and hereby authorise you to have hold and enjoy the said Dignity and Rank of an Honorary Officer of Our aforesaid Order together with all and singular the privileges thereunto belonging or appertaining.

**Given** at Our Court at Saint James's under Our Sign Manual and the Seal of Our said Order this Twelfth day of September 2005 in the Fifty-seventh year of Our Reign.

By the Sovereign's Command.

Grand Master

Grant of the Dignity of an Honorary Officer of the Civil Division of the Order of the British Empire to Mr. Om Puri

The Queen of the United Kingdom, Elizabeth II honoured Om by making him an officer of Order of the British Empire in 2005.

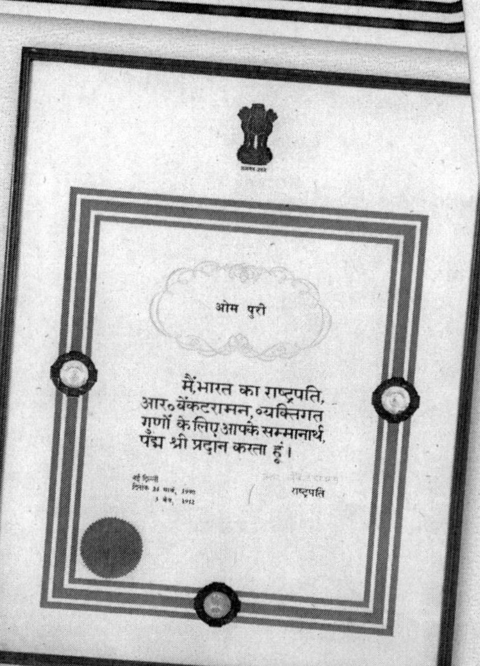

ओम पुरी

मैं, भारत का राष्ट्रपति, आर० वेंकटरामन, व्यक्तिगत गुणों के लिए आपके सम्मानार्थ, पद्म श्री प्रदान करता हूं।

नई दिल्ली

राष्ट्रपति

The Padma Shri Om received from the then president, R. Venkatraman, in 1990.

# Awards & Accolades

| YEAR | HONOUR |
|---|---|
| 1982 | National Award (Best Actor in *Arohan*) |
| 1983 | Filmfare Award (Best Supporting Actor in *Aakrosh*) |
| 1984 | National Award (Best Actor in *Ardh Satya*) |
| 1984 | Karlovy Vary Award (Best Actor in *Ardh Satya*) |
| 1986 | Soviet Land Nehru Award |
| 1989 | Padma Shri |
| 1997 | Crystal Star (Best Actor in *My Son the Fanatic*) |
| 1999 | BAFTA nomination (Best Actor in *East is East*) |
| 2000 | Grand Prix de Americans (Montreal Film Festival) |
| 2004 | Maharashtra Ratna |
| 2005 | OBE (Made an officer of the Order of the British Empire by HRH Queen Elizabeth II) |
| 2008 | Chairman, National Film Development Corporation (NFDC) |

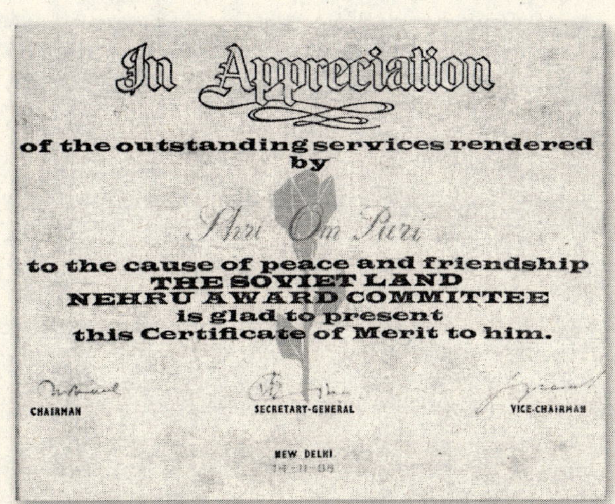

In Appreciation

of the outstanding services rendered
by

Shri Om Puri

to the cause of peace and friendship
THE SOVIET LAND
NEHRU AWARD COMMITTEE
is glad to present
this Certificate of Merit to him.

CHAIRMAN SECRETARY-GENERAL VICE-CHAIRMAN

NEW DELHI

The Soviet Land Nehru Award that Om won in 1986.

# Index